No More Plastic Jesus

ORBIS BOOKS

Maryknoll, New York 10545

NO MORE PLASTIC JESUS

Global Justice and Christian Lifestyle

ADAM DANIEL FINNERTY

Fifth Printing, August 1981

Copyright © 1977 Orbis Books, Maryknoll, New York 10545

Manufactured in the United States of America

Library of Congress Cataloging in Publication Data

Finnerty, Adam, 1944-
  No more plastic Jesus.

  Bibliography: p.
  SUMMARY: Discusses the seriousness of the worldwide dilemma of hunger, depletion of natural resources, and pollution and suggests ways to "reclaim the planet", particularly ways that the church as an institution can help and also ways responsive adults in adopting a simple, truly Christian lifestyle can contribute to global change.
  1. Simplicity. 2. Church and social problems.
3. Civilization, Modern—1950-   [1. Human ecology.
2. Environmental policy. 3. Church and social problems.
4. Conduct of life. 5. Civilization, Modern—
1950-   ] I. Title.
BJ1496.F5   261.8   76-13174
ISBN 088344-340-6
ISBN 0-88344-341-4 pbk.

To Frances, John,
and my brother, Tom

CONTENTS

vii

II. THE SIMPLE LIVING MOVEMENT

III. A LOOK AT THE CHURCH

iv. Summing It All Up

Appendixes

PREFACE

This book has its ideas and information drawn from three sources: my personal life, the work that I and others have done in the Simple Living movement, and the many excellent studies and papers that are available on the subject of our global crisis with respect to world hunger, the depletion of natural resources, and the pollution of the environment. So, perhaps like many books, it represents a fusion of pieces written at odd moments, inspirations, and ideas worked out in various contexts. Some of it was written at high speed, out of an urgent desire to communicate my own thoughts and experiences. Some of it was hammered out after long hours in the library, with notes, charts, and half-opened books scattered over the floor—and with me wondering if the next sentence, the next word even, would ever get written.

I say all this because I think it will make it easier to understand the book. Its style, its pacing, its degree of impersonality will vary. And yet it is all of a piece, because the theme—the present world situation and what I, you, we can do about it—sounds on every page.

It may be helpful for the reader to know a bit about me and the work I am now doing. But what to say? Well, to start with I'm an Air Force brat, my father having been a career employee in the Air Force, and I traveled around with the family (twenty-one different schools by the time I was finished and sixty different mailing addresses). My mother was a school teacher and a Protestant, my father a Catholic. I spent my first seven years as a Catholic, but after first grade found myself being taken to whatever Protestant church suited my mother's intellectual bent.

I grew up in small and medium-sized towns with friends and relations who could only be described as Middle American. In high school I read a lot of science fiction, got good grades, and believed everything my civics book said about America. Then I went to college.

That was in 1962. One year later, as I traveled north to school—the University of Pennsylvania—on a segregated railroad car, Martin Luther King's historic March on Washington was in progress. One year earlier John Kennedy had authorized the positioning of a few thousand "advisors" in a Southeast Asian country I had never heard of. When I first entered college, fraternities and sororities dominated the scene and a Saturday night drunk or a mini-riot after the football game was the most exciting kind of thing that happened on campus. By the time I left, our main administration building had weathered sit-ins and sieges, Dow recruiters had been prevented from getting anywhere near prospective employees. On the West Coast, Berkeley had flared up, Oakland had been the site of major antidraft riots; the Pentagon had been stormed, and everywhere people talked about the "long, hot summer" that had been or might be coming. In other words, I had come of age smack in the middle of the 1960s. And that was when my own activist involvement began—civil rights, the support of striking tenant farmers, the whole range of protest to end the war.

Of course, my generation could have done no other. All the values of the society we had been brought up in were being called into question: To be alive then was to be involved.

But this book is not an autobiography. The background I have sketched is mentioned because I feel that the reader will gain by having some sense of who I am and of the experiences that have shaped my life. Happily, for me, as for many of my generation, "getting it all together" has meant finding—or, more precisely, being found by—Jesus. And so, in searching for solutions to the world problems with which my book is concerned, I see Christianity playing a vital role—particularly Christianity in the radical simplicity that characterized its first centuries.

For incalculable assistance in the writing of this book, I am indebted to several religious fellowships with which I have been associated. First, Kirkridge, an ecumenical Christian conference and retreat center, on whose staff I found the "time in the wilderness" that enabled me to clarify my thinking, both intellectually and spiritually; then the Philadelphia Life Center, a radical pacifist community made up of some one hundred members living together in fifteen households. Although it is a secular community, it evolved from a Quaker base and thus has many of the attributes of a spiritual community; and its primary reason for being is to provide a center of support for people who want to change our society.

Of the company of like-minded people whose association gave rise to the Shakertown Pledge, a religiously grounded Simple Living commitment at the center of this book, the reader will learn much more in the chapters that follow. In January 1974 I began officially to function as the national organizer and secretary concerned with spreading the word about the Pledge. It meant traveling to campus and church gatherings, answering questions about global resources, consumption, personal change, and world reform. It meant study and writing.

Lastly, there is the Churchmouse Collective, a working group formed with religiously oriented comrades in addition to myself with the object of challenging the churches and religious people everywhere to commit themselves to bringing a better global society into being. Most of our activity thus far has been focused on running or facilitating workshops, seminars, and retreats on the subjects of simple living, community formation, and global justice. In the Churchmouse Collective, many of my own half-formed ideas have had a chance to develop and become clarified; challenged and supported by each other, we have all seen our individual visions grow and deepen. Moreover, as we have traveled around the country, we have found many people thinking along similar lines; so much so that we have begun to think of this loose network of concerned people as the beginnings of a radical religious Simple Living "movement" in the country.

Indeed, it is the growing Simple Living movement that has given this book its shape and tenor. What began as a personal and limited vision has grown through the challenge, the support, and the inspired thinking of many, many other people. It would be foolish to claim that the book is anything more than my own personal synthesis of the ideas and hopes that support the movement. And yet there is a very real sense in which it is not my book. My thanks are due to all these others.

Thanks are due, too, to John Eagleson, editor at Orbis Books, for encouraging me to write this book, and to Orbis Books for supporting me while I did so.

And thanks to all my friends and my family for their support through all my changes, my ups and downs, my withdrawals, my overbearing certainties.

INTRODUCTION

*"The principal hazards that man now faces are largely of his own making and largely within his own control."**
    —ROY AMARA, REPORT TO THE WORLD FUTURIST
             SOCIETY, JUNE 25, 1975

In recent years it has become somewhat fashionable to speak of the global situation in terms of the "ethics of the lifeboat." Advocates of this approach conjure up a picture of hard-pressed humanity, adrift in a hostile sea in an overcrowded lifeboat with too few supplies to go around. More lurid pictures have the lifeboat surrounded with desperate swimmers on the brink of death, clamoring and fighting to scramble on board and thus threatening to sink the boat entirely. This, the lifeboat ethicists tell us, is the realistic assessment of the world situation today: There are too many people and not enough resources, and we are simply going to have to let some people drown.

While such an image has a certain kind of graphic appeal and may suggest the philosophic acceptance of the inevitable to those of us who have secure seats in the lifeboat, its underlying assumption does not at all represent the considered judgment of the political and scientific community. On the contrary, most writers on the topic of world resources say that we

---

*While I have endeavored to use nonmasculine "universals" in my writing, in quoting other authors I have kept their original usage. My apologies to readers who are justly offended by such language—especially in publications of recent date.

1

do have the resources, the talent, and the technology to provide a decent life for all the world's people. "The fact of the matter is that today there is more than enough to go around for everyone if only it is properly planned, distributed, and consumed," says Victor Papanek, an international designer and educator who has worked closely with the United Nations Educational, Scientific and Cultural Organization in developing production and communications equipment for Third World needs.[1] Nobel prize winner Linus Pauling agrees: "The discoveries that scientists have made provide now the possibility of abolishing starvation and malnutrition, improving the well-being and enriching the lives of all the world's people."[2]

The Club of Rome, an international assemblage of business people, scientists, and planners who have made it their business to look realistically at world resources and development, concluded in their much-quoted first report:

It is possible to alter these growth trends and to establish a condition of ecological and economic stability that is sustainable far into the future. The state of global equilibrium could be designed so that the basic material needs of each person on earth are satisfied and each person has an equal opportunity to realize his individual human potential.[3]

Finally, our former secretary of state, Henry Kissinger, a man who is not noted for his utopianism or wooly-headed idealism, has concluded that improving the quality of life "has become a universal political demand, a technical possibility and a moral imperative."[4]

A far more realistic image of our embattled planet might be that of an ocean liner, rather than a lifeboat. This ocean liner, too, is in danger of sinking, but not so much because of the hordes of hungry passengers clinging to the rail and massed together in its dirty and dangerous holds as because of the deportment of the first-class passengers. These passengers, making up about 28 percent of the ship's list, have insisted on bringing along their automobiles, their freezers, their television sets, their kitchen disposal units, and their pets. A number of the ship's holds are filled with empty cans, bottles, discarded plastic, old newspapers, and broken appliances—all the residue of first-class consumption. In other sections there are cattle, which are periodically slaughtered to provide meat for the first-class passengers, and in still other compartments there is grain to feed the cattle. On the deck of the ship are amassed assorted tanks, airplanes, explosives, and a small army of guards, which the first-class passengers have brought along in order to assure themselves of a safe and undisturbed voyage.

To complete the picture we should note that the privileged passengers have some dangerous personal habits. They flush garbage down the toilets, blow tobacco smoke and shoot aerosol sprays into the ventilating system, and insist on unlimited use of the ship's limited electricity and water. Every once in a while they have a major brawl among themselves and threaten to sink the ship entirely. The ship has no captain, since the first-class passengers are afraid to give anyone authority to steer a new course or to change the ship's arrangements. Rather, there is a committee, which has no power and is not allowed access to the bridge, but permitted only to discuss possible future directions and make suggestions.

I would submit that this is not an unfair picture of the present condition of our planet. Others have used the imagery of a stagecoach, hurtling driverless down a steep canyon trail, or of a spaceship whose essential life-support systems are breaking down. Central to all these images is the realization that the vehicle is out of control, with consequent peril to all who are on board; central also is the assumption that the trouble has been caused by the foolish, selfish, and shortsighted behavior of the passengers. This twofold awareness, of danger and of responsibility, is reflected in our time in the communications media and in political programs.

It has become common for those of us in the rich world to be told how well we live and to have our affluence contrasted with the plight of the world's poor. Television shows babies starving in Africa, the newspapers tell of horrible conditions in the overcrowded cities and shantytowns, magazines carry heart-rending appeals to us to "adopt" a sad-eyed child. Behind so many of these portraits and appeals the message seems to be: "Look how well-off you are and how miserable it is for others. Why don't you give a little from your surplus to help these people?" In other words, it is an appeal to be charitable. It is based, it seems, on an assumption that there is nothing basically wrong with our lifestyle except that others cannot share it. One day, we are led to believe, the whole world may be able to enjoy a lifestyle like ours—provided that we are a little more generous in our private and public aid and in sharing our technological and organizational expertise with others.

This outlook is dead wrong. There *is* something basically the matter with the lifestyle of the rich world, and most especially of the United States; and if we do not change it drastically and soon, we may take the world beyond the limits wherein human life can be supported. The simple fact is that the planet is rapidly becoming less capable of sustaining the present lifestyle of the rich, and if the rest of the world were somehow brought up to our levels of production and consumption, we would all together strip the earth of its resources in less than ten years. The theory of gradual development that has been pushed by the rich world upon the poor is largely a myth. In the thirty years since the development concept was launched, there has been no substantial improvement in the lot of the poor in those nations which have been the recipients of our aid, and within the present workings of the international economic system *there never will be.*

Unless there are some major changes in our global production and distribution system, the prognosis for our ailing world is bad: The rich will continue to get richer and the poor to get poorer—or, at best, the poor will stay the same. That is, in the short-range outlook. In the long-range outlook—say, thirty to a hundred years—the prospects for the rich minority are likewise dim, because without some major change in their economies, it appears likely that they will either pollute themselves and the rest of the world out of existence or diminish the earth's resources to such an extent that they themselves will become incapable of sustaining their lifestyle and begin to regress.

This assessment is not based on the speculations of a few wild-eyed environmentalists; it is a growing consensus of many of the world's leading scientists, educators, and planners. It is shared by many astute and forward-looking politicians, and by major industrialists as well. Their informed opinion is that we must begin without delay to redirect the thrust of our production system. If we do not, they warn, it may prove too late.

It is the assumption of this book that these fears of global disaster are well-founded. It is also the assumption of this book that the situation is not hopeless. I shall endeavor to suggest how it will be possible for us to reclaim this planet and to forge an international society in which all people's basic needs are met. But first, in the chapters which follow, I shall attempt to spell out in more detail the shape and seriousness of our present global dilemma, focusing particularly on the economy of the United States and its relationship with the world-resource distribution system.

NOTES

1. *Design for the Real World* (New York: Bantam Books, 1973), p. 329.

2. *On the Developed and the Developing* (Santa Barbara, Cal.: Center for the Study of Democratic Institutions, 1965), p. 2.

3. Donella H. Meadows et al., *The Limits to Growth* (New York: Signet Books, 1972), p. 29.

4. Statement made in an address to the Special Assembly of the United Nations gathered to discuss the availability of raw materials; quoted by Anthony Lewis in the *New York Times,* April 18, 1974.

I. THE GLOBAL SITUATION

"The industrial way of life with its ethos of expansion is . . . not sustainable. Its termination within the lifetime of someone born today is inevitable—unless it continues to be sustained by an entrenched minority at the cost of imposing great suffering on the rest of mankind. We can be certain, however, that sooner or later it will end (only the precise time and circumstances are in doubt)."

—BLUEPRINT FOR SURVIVAL

1. The Limits to Consumption

If you are an American and come anywhere near what statisticians would call the "average," you are a very lucky person. You live in a house you probably own. It has 5.2 rooms which you share with 2.2 other people in your family. It has running water, electricity, a refrigerator, a vacuum cleaner, a telephone, a coffeemaker, and a host of other appliances, and it is worth $21,000. Even if you are a "poor American," the chances are excellent that you have indoor plumbing, heat, and electricity; there is a 77 percent chance that you have a television and a refrigerator and a 40 percent chance that you have a car.

As part of an average American family, you had an aggregate income last year of over $11,000. Your family has at least one car, and last year it spent $1,900 on food and $738 on recreation. If you are an adult, you spent $200 on alcohol last year and $120 on cigarettes. No matter what your age, your government is wealthy enough to spend $400 a year on your "defense."

You live in a country that has the highest standard of living in the world. You and your fellow citizens are 6 percent of the world's population, or 210 million people; but you consume 33 percent of the world's energy, 44 percent of the world's

9

newsprint, and you own 43 percent of its telephones and motor vehicles.

If you are a woman, the chances are good that you will live to be seventy-four years old; if a man, you are likely to live to be sixty-seven. You can expect to live that long because your country has a large and effective health establishment that has one hospital bed for every 133 persons and one doctor for every 634. Besides, your average caloric daily intake is 3,120, and good nourishment is the key to good health.[1]

If you are not an American, but happen to be a Soviet or a Japanese citizen, or a European, Australian, Canadian, New Zealander, or white South African, then you are still lucky. You are lucky because you have been born into a country that is part of the "upper class" in our world society. Together with the citizens of the United States, you constitute just slightly more than a billion people, or 28 percent of the world's population. But you are fortunate enough to be part of the group that possesses 80 percent of the world income. More specifically, your "class" divides up 84 percent of the world's energy, 93 percent of the world's telephones, 89 percent of the world's tractors, and 92 percent of the world's automobiles. Your combined countries expend $256 billion a year on their military budgets; and, in fact, these nations to which you belong have felt wealthy enough to spend over $4 trillion on war and war-preparedness since this century began.[2]

While your income, and thus your consumption level, is not likely to be as high as that of your counterpart in the United States, it is nevertheless probable that you live in an adequate house with running water and electricity, and that your diet is more than adequate. If you are lucky enough to be a Swede, you may live longer than your American brother or sister; and if you are an Italian, you have more hospital beds and doctors available to you when you are sick. But whatever one of the nations in this group you belong to, it is most likely that you can read and that your children will complete secondary school. It is also likely that you have some sort of motorized transportation available, that you live on a paved street, that your sewage is treated, and that your family includes at least one employed person.

LIVING ON THE BOTTOM

Now, suppose that you happen to be a citizen of the countries that contain the other 73 percent of the world's population. Then you are not so lucky. If you are a Pakistani, the chances are ten to one that even if this sentence were written in your native language you could not read it. If you are a Pakistani parent, there is an 80 percent chance that your child is undernourished and a 25 percent chance that any new children you have will die before their fifth birthday. If you are a Nigerian, there is a 77 percent chance that you live in a one-room shack, with no water or electricity. You can look forward to a lifetime of about thirty-seven years, and if you get sick you have to compete with 43,469 other people for a doctor. As a Ghanian, you will be able to count only 8.5 radios for every hundred members of your country's population; as an Indian, 2.3. (The United States figure is 169 radios for every 100 people; that's right, 169.)

In your world of 2.5 billion people, 700 million—or over half the adult population—are illiterate. The "most conservative" estimate by the United Nations is that 400 million of you are undernourished, and the Food and Agriculture Organization estimates that every day 15,000 of your people die from starvation. It is estimated that one-half billion of your adults are unemployed or grossly underemployed, and that over a billion of you live on the equivalent of $4 a week each. Your total average yearly income is about $200, or just about what an average American adult spends on liquor in a year.[3]

FROM STATISTICS TO REALITY

Statistics are sometimes a difficult medium for conveying reality. It is, for instance, unlikely that anyone reading this book owns a house with 5.2 rooms, or 1.7 radios, or half a TV.

Nor is it easy to form a picture of the life of a Bolivian peasant child by becoming aware that an American child is seventy times more likely to attend college. It may be helpful, therefore, to add to this initial survey of the world situation by availing ourselves of a few portraits of life in the developing world as it has been represented by recent newspaper and television coverage.

—Allah Dad, aged forty-three, begins his day with a breakfast of bread and tea. He then walks four miles to a grassy area near some government buildings, where he sits or kneels and cuts grass for seven hours. When the grass is gathered, he takes it home to feed his family's water buffalo. If the grass is green, his buffalo will give about twenty pounds of milk. This milk, when sold, will bring in ninety-five cents, or just about enough for his family of seven to live on for another day. Mr. Dad, a Pakistani and a devout Moslem, believes that it is "Allah's will" that he is so poor. He hopes that his son will do better than he has, and thus he spends fifty cents a week to send him to school.

—Pitung, an Indonesian who has no other name and doesn't know his age, lives in a cardboard shack near the railroad tracks in Jakarta. He came here from his village, where jobs are scarce and seasonal, because he could no longer make a living. He has no land and no savings. In fact, except for the clothes on his back and his floppy hat, anything he owns could be carried in his pocket. The sixty shacks in the little community of which he is a member house some four hundred people, most of whom barely stay alive from day to day by picking trash, doing odd jobs, and begging. Jakarta has grown to be a city of five million from a beginning at one-tenth of that population thirty years ago. Eighty percent of its people live in conditions similar to Pitung's—some a little better, some worse. In 1970 the city government declared Jakarta offically closed to new arrivals, yet newcomers trickle in every day. Periodically government troops show up at Pitung's settlement and burn the shacks down. The inhabitants are taken to the edge of the town and told to go back to their villages.

Most return to the city, since survival is even more difficult in the rural areas.

—In New Delhi, scores of young women are working at the site of a new tourist hotel. Their job is to carry large bowls of concrete and stone on their heads to another part of the project where walls are being erected. The loads are fifty pounds or more and they do this work steadily for nine hours a day, six days a week. It is said that only women twenty-five years of age or under can do the job because it is so physically taxing. For this work the women earn fifty cents a day. This is just enough to pay their rent and buy their food. When they are interviewed, it is discovered that these women have come up to New Delhi from Southern India. They were lured here by the promise of good pay, and were given a one-way ticket. Many of them hoped to earn enough money to send some to their families. But now they make just enough to survive, and few can even hope to earn enough money for their ticket back.

—High in the mountains of Bolivia, two miners are straining to push a cart loaded with tin ore. Their work is hard and dirty and is made all the more difficult by the cold air and high altitude. The ore they are mining will be sent to smelters in the United States or Great Britain, where it may wind up as a tin can. These miners, who earn the equivalent of 25 dollars a month, will probably never eat anything that comes in a tin can. Nearby a little girl and her brother trudge along the tracks. Her legs are wrapped in rags and her arms are blue from the cold. She is there hoping to collect ore that may have dropped from the cart. If the ore is good, it can be exchanged in a black market store for some food. The girl is about six years old. Her brother is about four.

—Finally, a mental exercise developed by the economist Robert Heilbroner:

We must conjure up in our mind's eye what underdevelopment means for the two billion human beings for whom it is not a statistic but a living experience of daily life. . . . It is not easy to make this mental jump. But let us attempt it by imagining how a typical American family, living in a small suburban house . . . , could be transformed into an equally typical family of the underdeveloped world.

We begin by invading the house of our imaginary American family to strip it of its furniture. Everything goes: beds, chairs, tables, television sets, lamps. We will leave the family with a few old blankets, a kitchen table, a wooden chair. Along with the bureaus go the clothes. Each member of the family may keep in his wardrobe his oldest suit or dress, a shirt or blouse. We will permit a pair of shoes to the head of the family, but none for the wife or children.

We move into the kitchen. The appliances have already been taken out, so we turn to the cupboards and larder. The box of matches may stay, a small bag of flour, some sugar and salt. A few moldy potatoes already in the garbage can must be hastily rescued, for they will provide much of tonight's meal. We will leave a handful of onions, and a dish of dried beans. All the rest we take away: the meat, the fresh vegetables, the canned goods, the crackers, the candy.

Now we have stripped the house: the bathroom has been dismantled, the running water shut off, the electric wires taken out. Next we take away the house. The family moves to the toolshed. . . .

Communications must go next. No more newspapers, magazines, books—not that they are missed, since we must take away the family's literacy as well. . . .

Now government services must go. No more postman, no more fireman. There is a school, but it is three miles away and consists of two classrooms. They are not too overcrowded since only half the children in the neighborhood go to school. There are, of course, no hospitals or doctors nearby. The nearest clinic is ten miles away and is tended by a midwife. It can be reached by bicycle, provided that the family has a bicycle, which is unlikely. Or one can go by bus—not always inside, but there is usually room on top.

Finally, money. We will allow our family a cash hoard of five dollars. . . .

Meanwhile, the head of our family must earn his keep. As a peasant cultivator with three acres to tend, he may raise the equivalent of $100 to $300 worth of crops a year. If he is a tenant farmer, which is more than likely, a third or so of his crop will go to his landlord and probably another ten percent to the local money lender. . . .

And so we have brought our typical American family down to the very bottom of the human scale. It is, however, a bottom in which we can find, give or take a hundred million souls, at least a billion people.[4]

THE PERILS OF CONSUMPTION

The United States is the consumption capital of the world. With a gross national product that is now over one trillion dollars a year, American citizens enjoy the highest standard of living in the world (see tables 1 and 2 for some comparisons). Disposable income in the United states in 1973 was a staggering $882.5 billion, or $4,202 per person. In that same year our federal government spent 407.1 billion to defend us, provide us with roads, and insure our welfare. That expenditure comes out to an additional $1,938 for every person.[5]

In addition to our 354 million radios, our 117 million motor vehicles, our 99 million television sets, and our 68 million vacuum cleaners, we traveled 66.6 billion miles by air, put 2 billion barrels of gasoline into our cars, and utilized 577 pounds of packaging materials per person on an annual basis.[6]

We are far and away the leader of the world's consumption parade. Whereas other nations may belong to the same weal-

Table 1
IF THE WORLD POSSESSED AT THE CURRENT UNITED STATES LEVEL

Item	U. S. Holdings	World Holdings if Raised to U. S. Rate	Multiple of Present World Holdings
Tractors	4.39 million	73.3 million	7
Telephones	131 million	2.2 billion	7
Motor vehicles (passenger and commercial)	117 million	2 billion	7
Radios	354 million	5.9 billion	NA*
Television sets	99 million	1.7 billion	NA
Electric blankets	37.4 million	625 million	NA
Electric coffee makers	65.8 million	1.1 billion	NA
Refrigerators	69.3 million	1.2 billion	NA
Vacuum cleaners	67.9 million	1.1 billion	NA

Source: Author's computations based on data from Statistical Yearbook, 1973 (New York: United Nations, 1974) and Statistical Abstract of the United States, 1974 (Washington, D.C.: United States Department of Commerce, 1974).
* Current world holdings not available for comparison.

thy club, we are unquestionably its foremost members. For example, the average citizen of the Soviet Union or Japan has slightly over one-fourth of the income that we do, the average (West) German about half.[7] Using per capita energy consumption as an indicator of overall goods consumption, we can boast that ours is more than six times the world average. That is just about twice the consumption of an Australian or Swede and more than sixty times that of an Indian or Ghanian.[8]

A lifestyle of such excellence, however, requires a lot of resources. Our automobiles, for example, require 15 percent of the world's annual petroleum production for their man-

Table 2
IF THE WORLD CONSUMED
AT THE CURRENT UNITED STATES ANNUAL LEVEL

Item	U. S. Level of Consumption	World Level of Consumption	World Level Raised to U. S. Rate	Multiple of Present World Consumption
Energy	2.4 billion metric tons of coal equivalent	7.4 billion metric tons	40.5 billion metric tons	5.5
Steel	138 million metric tons	617 million metric tons	2.3 billion metric tons	3.7
Tin	54,000 metric tons	191,000 metric tons	908,000 metric tons	4.7
Rubber	3 million metric tons	7.7 million metric tons	49.7 million metric tons	6.4
Newsprint	9.4 million metric tons	21.4 million metric tons	157 million metric tons	7.3
Nitrogen fertilizer	7.6 million metric tons	36 million metric tons	126 million metric tons	3.5
Beer	164.7 million hectolitres	678.6 million hectolitres	2.75 trillion hectolitres	4.1
Defense spending	$78.3 billion	$272 billion	$1.3 trillion	4.8

Source: Author's computations based on data from Statistical Yearbook, 1973 (New York: United Nations, 1974) and Statistical Abstract of the United States, 1974 (Washington, D.C.: United States Department of Commerce, 1974).

ufacture and operation.[9] Our daily newspaper requires 9.4 million metric tons of newsprint a year, or 44 percent of the world's supply. In fact, to support our way of life, we consume 28 tons of materials from fields, forests, mines, and waters of the world for each person each year.[10] No wonder, then, that when world consumption statistics are gathered it is found that our 6 percent of the world's population has claimed in a given year 42 percent of the world's aluminum production, 33 percent of the world's petroleum production and 25 percent of the annual lead production. Overall, it is estimated that the people of the United States require about 33 percent of the world's raw material production to service their needs.[11]

Now the trouble is that this level of consumption is not sustainable. World resources are not infinitely available; in fact, they are limited. As table 3 shows, if the rest of the world were to attempt to live at our level of consumption, *all known reserves* of petroleum, tin, zinc, natural gas, lead, copper, tungsten, gold, and mercury would have *disappeared entirely within ten years*. And this computation is simply based on multiplying present consumption rates for the world as a whole by a factor

Table 3
DEPLETION OF KNOWN WORLD RESOURCES CALCULATED AT VARIOUS RATES OF CONSUMPTION

Item	At Current Rate	At Growth Rate	If World Consumption Raised to U. S. Rate
Aluminum	100 yrs.	31 yrs.	14.3 yrs.
Copper	36 yrs.	21 yrs.	6.6 yrs.
Lead	26 yrs.	21 yrs.	6.2 yrs.
Iron	240 yrs.	93 yrs.	51.4 yrs.
Petroleum	31 yrs.	20 yrs.	5.6 yrs.
Tin	17 yrs.	15 yrs.	4.3 yrs.
Zinc	23 yrs.	18 yrs.	5.3 yrs.
Natural Gas	38 yrs.	22 yrs.	3.6 yrs.

Source: Author's computations based on data from Donella H. Meadows et al., *The Limits to Growth* (New York: Signet, 1972), pp. 64–67.

which raises them to United States per capita levels of consumption. To provide an array of newspapers, automobiles, telephones, and electrical gadgets similar to that enjoyed by the American would call for the construction of thousands of factories, millions of miles of roads and railroads, thousands of electrical generating plants, millions of schools and training facilities—the list goes on and on. This, one expert has concluded, would require a hundred or two hundred times present world resource production levels. In other words, given present world resource reserves, such an undertaking is actually impossible.[12]

What this means, in pure and simple language, is that the United States is grossly and dangerously overconsuming world resources. Average Americans, because of their high level of material satisfaction, are not models to be emulated but to be avoided and condemned. *The world cannot afford our lifestyle;* and, as I shall show in a moment, every year that we continue to live the way we do is another year of diminished resources and thus of diminished hope.

When the Club of Rome, to which we referred earlier, commissioned a study of the prospects for the future, they found that if industrial growth were allowed to continue unabated, the inevitable results would be massive air and water pollution, severe famines, and probably economic collapse.[13] Their study pointed out that world industrial growth has proceeded apace throughout this century and is currently adding a 7 percent increase in demand on world resources every year.[14] As another study has concluded, this means that total demand on the ecosphere will be up six times by the year 2000.[15]

Table 3 shows in graphic terms what the cost of growth can be. From this table, which was drawn from data provided in *The Limits to Growth,* it can be seen that some commodities are in danger of being exhausted by current consumption rates. When the "growth rate" for these materials is figured (by adding the average annual increase in demand), it can be seen that they are exhausted even sooner. Known reserves of zinc, for example, can be expected to last for 23 years at present rates, but only 18 years at the growth rate. Iron, which would last for 240 years at present rates, will be exhausted in 93 years at the growth rate.

Even given the best in recycling systems, the latest pollution control technology, and a successful program of world population control, the Club of Rome study still concludes that unlimited growth will bring systemic collapse within the lifetimes of our children.[16]

It is important to recognize that the bulk of world growth, in quantitative terms, comes from the expanding production and consumption of the rich nations. Since they divide between them a fantastically disproportionate share of world resources, they are also the nations responsible for the world's growth rate. If energy comsumption is taken as a good estimate of the level of resource demand (and most experts feel this is realistic), then since the richest 28 percent divide up 84 percent of the world's energy it is likely that they also account for 84 percent or more of the world's growth. Furthermore, since their consumption level is already so high, it can be reasonably surmised that the average rich-world child, during his or her lifetime, will have a negative impact on the earth's environment fourteen to twenty-five times as great as that of the average poor-world child.

THE QUESTION OF POLLUTION

If the expansion of world consumption presents a gloomy picture from the standpoint of limited world resources, the outlook is even more dismal when pollution is taken into account. Even at current levels of industrial production, there are many who question whether we have already dug two-thirds of our way into an environmental grave.

Here are some illustrations from the world scene today:

—World wildlife experts estimate that air and water pollution is threatening 350 bird, 280 mammal, and 20,000 plant species with extinction.[17]

—World combustion of fossil fuels has added six billion

tons of carbon monoxide to the atmosphere. Weather experts are concerned with the prospect that continued additions of carbon monoxide will create a "greenhouse effect," trapping greater amounts of the sun's heat in our atmosphere. This could cause the partial melting of the polar icecaps and flood our coastal cities.[18]

—Indiscriminate dumping of sewage and pollution by phosphates from detergents, DDT and pesticides from the fields, and chemicals and debris from industrial production are threatening the world's surface waters with destruction. More than one-third of United States lakes are showing signs of "cultural eutrophication"—that is, they are dying.[19] And here are reports on two other large bodies of water:

The Baltic is a dying sea. Poisoned by DDT, mercury and oil, contaminated by industrial waste, particularly from the wood-pulping industries, and municipal sewage of Sweden, Finland, Russia, and Poland, there are now many areas where all fish life is dead. What fish are caught in the Baltic have been so contaminated with DDT that they have had to be condemned.[20]

San Francisco Bay once provided 15 million pounds of oysters and 300,000 pounds of clams a year. Neither can be found today. Shrimps are still harvested, but only 10,000 pounds instead of six and a half million annually. In the words of the *UNESCO Courier*, of March 1969, San Francisco Bay "exists largely as a giant cesspool, a garbage dump."[21]

—The oceans of the world are receiving a terrific load of sludge and chemical waste. It is estimated that two million metric tons of oil are leaked or spilled into the oceans every year, most of it from "normal" operations.[22] Lead concentrates in the Pacific off the coast of California have increased ten times since tetraethyl lead was introduced into American gasoline.[23] Scientists are also worried about the effects of rising DDT levels in the oceans, since photosynthesis might be impaired and the oceans account for seventy percent of the atmosphere's oxygen supply.[24]

—Industrial and automobile combustion of fossil fuels is adding massive amounts of particles to the air, increasing the density of dust. Enormous amounts of oxides of sulfur and nitrogen are likewise added. In the ten years between 1957 and 1967 there was a 30 percent increase in the density of dust over the Pacific ocean.[25] The United States alone pours 143 million tons of pollutants into the air, 60 percent of which come from automobile exhausts.[26] This has meant an annual loss to the economy of $16.1 billion in the deterioration of materials, crop losses, and cleaning bills.[27] It also means a major loss in terms of health, with an increase in respiratory diseases and cancer and a lowered life expectancy. Louis Fuller, Air Pollution Control District Officer for the City of Los Angeles, said in a recent interview: "It is my opinion that the rate at which our atmosphere, our breathable air, is being contaminated is such that we do not have fifty years before cities are unlivable. I think we will be very lucky if we have twenty-five."[28]

If the present environmental crisis is frightening, it is nothing compared with what we will shortly bring about if industrial growth continues. Ever increasing production means ever greater amounts of pesticides, carbon monoxide, sulfur dioxide, phosphorus, and other foreign elements introduced into the environment. A breakdown of the world growth in production for the fifteen-year period 1951–1966 is shown in table 4.

Table 4
WORLD GROWTH RATES FOR SELECTED ACTIVITIES

Activity	Rate of Annual Increase
Agriculture	3%
Industry based on farm products	6
Mineral production (including fuel)	5
Industry based on mineral production	9
Construction and Transportation	6

Source: *Man's Impact on the Global Environment:* Report of the Study of Critical Environmental Problems (Cambridge: Massachusetts Institute of Technology, 1970), p. 117.

A comparison of certain developed countries yields the following annual growth rates for the period 1950–1971: United States, 3.6 percent; Japan, 9.6 percent; Italy, 5.4 percent; (West) Germany, 6.5 percent.[29]

The best way to obtain a picture of what continued growth at these rates might mean in terms of the environment is to look at some present and projected figures for the United States, which with its seemingly modest growth rate of 3.6 percent can nevertheless be expected to contribute mightly to the world's pollution load.

At this very moment, without any further additions due to growth, the people of the United States are staggering under a burden of pollution and refuse that stuns the imagination. Every year we spend $4.5 billion to collect and dispose of 1.1 billion tons of mineral wastes, 110 million tons of industrial trash, and 250 million tons of household, commercial, and municipal wastes.[30] Every year we discharge 143 million tons of pollutants into the air. Every year 260 million pounds of phosphates and 511 million pounds of nitrogen reach our surface waters from municipal sewage alone.[31] Every year our paper production dumps 1.8 trillion gallons of water into our rivers, loaded with debris and suspended particles (which increases oxygen demand and thus kills plants and fish).[32]

And, as if this were not already enough, the prospect is for ever increasing amounts.

In 1971 a group of top scientists set out to assess what the environmental impact of continued United States growth would be. They based their calculations on a Ford Foundation financed study of American consumption trends. This study, published in 1963 as *Resources in America's Future,* had been an attempt to project national consumption levels until the year 2000.[33] Eight years later, the second group, whose study was published as *The Environmental Side Effects of Rising Industrial Output,* found that the *Resources* group had, if anything, slightly underestimated the pace of American growth. The projections of the *Resources* group for the period 1970 to 2000 are summarized in table 5.

From this table it can be seen that electric power generation is expected to increase by six times, automobile ownership by three times (to a total of 243.5 million vehicles), and petroleum and paper consumption to be up by a factor of three. What this meant, our environmental researchers discovered, was a staggering projection for ecological impact. Without the introduction of new and sophisticated pollution-control technology, the United States environment could be expected to sustain a threefold waste increase from steel and paper pro-

Table 5
PROJECTED INCREASES IN UNITED STATES CONSUMPTION
1970–2000

Item	1970	2000
Population	201 million	300+ million
Paper	40 million metric tons	135 million metric tons
Cars and passenger vehicles	83.3 million	243.5 million
Air passenger miles	66.6 million miles	225 billion miles
Packaging materials per capita	504 lbs.	633 lbs.
Household appliances	$13.4 billion	$56.8 billion
Furniture and furnishings	$12.5 billion	$35.6 billion
Electrical power generation	845 billion kilowatt hrs.	4.7 trillion kilowatt hrs.
Cooling water needed for energy production	57.3 billion gallons	204.7 billion gallons
Nuclear generating plants	37	900
High level nuclear waste (cumulative)	.8 million gallons	118 million gallons

Source: Author's computations based on data from H.H. Lansberg et al., *Resources in America's Future* (Baltimore, Md.: Johns Hopkins, 1963) and *Environmental Side Effects of Rising Industrial Output*, ed. J. Van Tassel (Lexington, Mass.: Heath, 1971).

duction, a two and one-half increase in pollution from petroleum production, and a sixfold pollution increase from chemicals manufacturing.[34] If autos continued to pollute at their
1966 levels, they would be injecting almost three hundred
million tons of pollutants into the air by the year 2000.[35]

Even more frightening was their projection of a pollution
threat that is relatively new, that of high-level nuclear wastes.
The nuclear plants that are supposed to be built by the year
2000 will account for half of all electricity generated and will
produce 118 million gallons of nuclear waste by that time. The
scientists point out that "highly dangerous to living cells, such
wastes cannot be dispersed, but instead are concentrated to
sludge to reduce bulk and are stored in shielded, isolated
tanks. . . ."[36] Thus, by the year 2000 it will be necessary for
the United States to have found suitable storage space for 118
million gallons of sludge, storage space that is virtually leak-
proof for an estimated twenty-five thousand years. One leak
from these dangerous wastes could conceivably destroy vast
areas and endanger huge portions of our ecosystem.

Even with the best pollution technology, the picture for the
United States in the year 2000 is not bright. Without what the
researchers call "drastic measures," our outlook is for an
increasing pollution of our air, water, and land. Our ever-
expanding consumption and subsequent discarding of automobiles, household appliances, plastics, bottles, aluminum
cans, and newspapers will threaten to bury us all in a mound
of refuse. And our cities may become vast sinkholes of dust
and carbon monoxide.

But our examination is not limited to the United States
alone. The United States was selected only to serve as a por-
tent of things to come. Imagine, then, an environmental impact of a sixfold nature on a world scale! J. George Harrar,
former president of the Rockefeller Foundation, has tried to
imagine it, and his conclusion is that "as all nations increasingly industrialize and as their cities burgeon, the possibility of
eventual suffocation as a result of this pollution becomes a
very real threat."[37]

However, as has been pointed out earlier, the danger involved in industrial growth is twofold. Left unchecked, it threatens not only to poison us and our atmosphere but also to · exhaust the very materials that feed its factories. The researchers who studied America's increased demand did not ask themselves whether the world had enough resources to sustain such levels of consumption. Nor did they ask whether it was fair for Americans to continue to lead lives of such reckless affluence.

In 1972 an eminent group of British scientists reviewed the data on world growth and pollution and issued their report under the title *Blueprint for Survival*, which we have frequently cited. Their conclusion:

The industrial way of life with its ethos of expansion is . . . not sustainable. Its termination within the lifetime of someone born today is inevitable—unless it continues to be sustained by an entrenched minority at the cost of imposing great suffering on the rest of mankind. We can be certain, however, that sooner or later it will end (only the precise time and circumstances are in doubt).[38]

However pessimistic the tone of the last few pages may seem, the purpose of this discussion is not to prove that the world is incapable of supporting its people. On the contrary, it is my firm belief, and the belief of many others, that with proper planning and distribution this planet is fully capable of providing a decent and sustainable life for the entire human race. To quote the Club of Rome:

It is possible to alter these growth trends and to establish a condition of ecological and economic stability that is sustainable far into the future. The state of global equilibrium could be designed so that the basic material needs of each person on earth are satisfied and each person has an equal opportunity to realize his individual human potential.[39]

The Club's researchers further conclude that with proper determination and cooperative planning, it would be possible to provide an environmentally sustainable living standard, comparable to that of present-day Europe, for a world population of some six billion people.[40] The many ways in which the present system of production and resource allocation can be reorganized for greater human benefit will be the subject of future chapters. There must be a willingness of the world's people to cooperate, and especially a willingness on the part of the affluent sectors to sacrifice short-term advantage for long-term gain. With this in mind, we shall now take a closer look at our global economy.

NOTES

1. Data for this portrait drawn from *Statistical Yearbook, 1973* (New York: United Nations Department of Economic and Social Affairs, 1974) and *Statistical Abstract of the United States, 1974* (Washington, D.C.: United States Department of Commerce, 1974).

2. Richard A. Falk, *This Endangered Planet* (New York: Vintage, 1972), p. 127.

3. Data drawn from United Nations *Statistical Yearbook, 1973,* and *Statistical Abstract of the United States, 1974.*

4. Robert Heilbroner, *The Great Ascent* (New York: Harper, 1963), pp. 33–37.

5. *Statistical Abstract of the United States, 1974,* p. 373.

6. See Alfred J. Van Tassel, ed., *Environmental Side Effects of Rising Industrial Output* (Lexington, Mass.: Heath, 1971), pp. 251, 196; see also Albert J. Fritsch, *The Contrasumers* (New York: Praeger, 1974), p. 107.

7. Meadows et al., *The Limits to Growth,* p. 49.

8. Fritsch, *The Contrasumers,* pp. 178–179.

9. Ibid., p. 26

10. Ibid., p. 23.

11. Meadows et al., *The Limits to Growth,* pp. 64–67.

12. Editors of *The Ecologist, Blueprint for Survival* (New York: Signet Books, 1972), p. 114.

13. Meadows et al., *The Limits to Growth.*

14. Ibid., p. 45.

15. Editors of *The Ecologist, Blueprint for Survival,* p. 5.

16. Meadows et al., *The Limits to Growth,* p. 29.

17. Editors of *The Ecologist, Blueprint for Survival,* p. 9.

18. Cecil E. Johnson, ed., *Eco-Crisis* (New York: Wiley, 1970), p. 127.

19. Ibid., p. 152.

20. Lynette Hamblin, *Pollution: The World Crisis* (London: Stacey, 1970), p. 32.

21. Ibid., p. 33.

22. *Man's Impact on the Global Environment,* Report of the Study of Critical Environmental Problems (Cambridge: Massachusetts Institute of Technology, 1970), p. 267.

23. Hamblin, *Pollution,* p. 31.

24. Falk, *This Endangered Planet,* p. 197.

25. Johnson, *Eco-Crisis,* p.127.

26. Ibid., p. 125.

27. Fritsch, *The Contrasumers,* p. 60.

28. Don Widner, *Timetable for Disaster* (Los Angeles: Nash, 1970), p. 249.

29. *Statistical Abstract of the United States, 1974,* p. 374.

30. Johnson, *Eco-Crisis,* p. 135.

31. Ibid., p. 156.

32. Van Tassel, *Environmental Side Effects,* p. 7.

33. H.H. Lansberg, L.I. Fishman, and J.L. Fisher, *Resources in America's Future* (Baltimore: Johns Hopkins, 1963).

34. Van Tassel, *Environmental Side Effects,* p. 74.

35. Ibid., p. 170.

36. Ibid., p. 138.

37. Johnson, *Eco-Crisis,* p. 124.

38. Editors of *The Ecologist, Blueprint for Survival,* p. 3.

39. Meadows et al., *The Limits to Growth,* p. 29.

40. Ibid., p. 171.

2. Global Waste

As we turn to the analysis of our global problems, it will perhaps be helpful (and less productive of debilitating guilt and anxiety) if we can think of the planet in terms of "systems design." Looking at our global system, we can see at once that there are several situations in urgent need of our attention. The environment is rapidly deteriorating, animal life is threatened, and great numbers of the human beings in the system lack the necessities of life. It is at the same time apparent that our system has the resources, the people-power, and the skills necessary to meet everyone's needs and preserve the biosphere. At present, to use a deliberately neutral term, our system is *poorly designed*. What we need, then, is a scheme of *global redesign* that can provide some clear direction for our applied energies.

Such an approach allows for some optimism about the future. Analysis shows that our present system has a tremendous number of potential areas for meaningful change and that we have the resources we need to bring into being a system of global balance and global justice. The chief ingredients which will be required are not more technology, or more tin or tungsten or any other natural resource, but a determination to change and a willingness to sacrifice short-term advantage for long-term goals.

Under the heading of poor design are three areas I would like to consider: (1) military spending, (2) planned obsolescence and other consumer stategies in the United States economy, and (3) Third World imitation of "First World" practices and the subservience of the developing countries' economies to those of the developed countries. Some attention to these three areas of poor design will be of assistance as we attempt to make a beginning, at least, at a systemic analysis of our global problems. It may also stimulate some thinking about how differently things might be done in the future.

MILITARY SPENDING

When we look at our global society with all its areas of dire poverty and urgent need, surely the billions of dollars that are expended yearly on armaments and military preparedness stand out as glaring examples of systemic waste. World expenditure for arms now runs over $200 billion a year, about $60 for every person in the world. This annual expenditure is the equivalent in dollar value of a year's income produced by the 1.8 billion people who make up the poorer half of the population. Think of it in contrast to the estimated $3 per person that the rich countries devote annually to foreign aid.

It has been realistically estimated that the nations of the world have expended about $1.5 trillion on arms since World War II. The United States and the Soviet Union, of course, represent the largest share of this expenditure, but even countries that are desperately poor have entered the arms race. Think of all the steel, aluminum, copper, electricity, petroleum, and countless other resources which have gone into the manufacture of military equipment in the last thirty years. Imagine what it would have meant if those resources and that productive capacity had been utilized to provide agricultural machinery, tools, housing, and medical and educational equipment for the world's poor people.

Of even greater significance is the amount of creative human energy that has gone into arms production—the millions of hours of human brain power and problem-solving ability that have been devoted to developing better ways to kill others. Imagine what the effect might be if, instead, all the creative talents of the engineers, business people, planners, designers, administrators, and scientists involved in the world military complex had been devoted to a global effort to improve the living conditions of the world's people. What a different world we might have today!

There have been many good studies of the world armament race and many excellent proposals for reducing or eliminating this wasteful expenditure of world resources and talent. I do not intend to repeat those proposals here; I simply desire to make this point: In any large-scale attempt to bring into being a more just global system, the world armaments race should be first on the agenda for radical system redesign. We must envision and then work for a world system which will eliminate this socially detrimental form of resource use, making it possible to transfer the energies and talents that have been applied to this area to more useful fields of research and application.

THE UNITED STATES ECONOMY:
PLANNED OBSOLESCENCE AND OTHER ANOMALIES

The United States of America, the world's wealthiest country and the linchpin of the global economy, is the seat of a production and distribution system that is massively, staggeringly, wasteful. And it is designed to be that way. To quote industrial designer J. Gordon Lippincott;

My mother had the same washing machine for twenty years. She has the same refrigerator now that she had when I went to high school thirty years ago. . . . We built a "leisure house" five years ago. . . . We're on our second washing machine and our second dryer. . . . We threw out the disposal. . . . We're on our third vacuum cleaner.[1]

The American economic system is deliberately based on waste. It is essentially the direct opposite of what an ecological production and distribution system might be, and it has put our economy on a collision course with the environment and with the needs of the world's poor. Day after day the American people are encouraged to buy, to consume, and to throw away. Advertisement and style-consciousness encourage us to seek the new and to discard present items well before their useful life is expended. Planned obsolescence creates products that are designed to fall apart and need early replacement. Not only are recycling and reusability—principles that are the hallmark of any ecologically sound system—not planned into our production; they are strongly resisted by manufacturers and designers. Each year new technologies, many of which are far more polluting than the technologies they have replaced, are causing our environment to deteriorate faster than our production has increased. And engineers and industrial designers concentrate their efforts on gimmicks and style changes rather than on durability, dependability, and safe use.

Most of us are aware that all these faults exist somewhere in our production system, but few realize just how wasteful and poorly designed our entire production system is from the point of view of environmental needs and the husbanding of resources. Perhaps even fewer realize that this systematic waste is a central and, some feel, necessary part of our entire economy.

Any sane and ecological production and distribution system would be governed by the following principles: First, products should be designed and manufactured to last as long as possible, be easily repaired, and be capable of being either recycled or turned to other uses after their primary purpose is ended. Second, research and design efforts should be focused on creating ever more useful, more durable, and cheaper products for the mass-consumption market. Third, no new technologies or products would be introduced to the public that have a significantly detrimental effect on the environment unless a very great need for them could be established. None of these principles currently holds sway in our system, and it is unlikely that, without major redesign, they ever will. The simple fact is that if we tried to introduce the first two —durability and serviceability—it would destroy our economy.

Planned Obsolescence

In Sacramento, California, Mike Tonis, aged eighty-one, drives around the city in a blue Model-T Ford. He has had the car for forty-one years; it has been driven over 700,000 miles and is still going strong. Every day, Mike told the Associated Press reporter who interviewed him, he gets offers to buy the car. But he says he turns them all down. The car runs fine, it rarely gives him trouble, and it is easy to repair.

Imagine if, forty years ago, automobile manufacturers had decided to bend their efforts to turn out an ideal car—one that was safe, dependable, cheap, and easy to repair, and that would last as long as, or longer than, the car Mike Tonis is so lucky to own. Imagine that other manufacturers—of appliances, of commercial equipment, of clothing—had decided to do the same. It isn't very much a matter of conjecture that the industries involved would soon have a very slow market for their products. Nor is it sheer conjecture to suppose that American consumers, if they were supplied with the basic products needed for a comfortable life, would elect to spend less money, go less into debt, and save more for the future.

But any modern economist could tell you that the scheme projected above is a never-failing formula for a deep economic depression. It is consumption that keeps our economy going, and when that tapers off or slows down, factories find themselves with surplus stock, workers get laid off, plant production is decreased, investment is slowed, and the whole economy begins to go downhill. Since the Great Depression it has become common wisdom that when such a sequence of events occurs, the quickest cure is to boost consumption.

During the 1958 recession, for example, the following dialogue occurred when President Eisenhower was asked at a press conference what the American people could do to help end it:

"A.—Buy."
"Q.—Buy what?"
"A.—Anything."[2]

Thus when President Nixon wanted to get the economy out of trouble in the early '70s, he authorized a cut in the federal excise tax on automobiles. President Ford later followed suit by allowing a $200 personal rebate on federal income taxes for 1974. The purpose was to get the American people to buy.

It seems to be a peculiar and enduring feature of our economic system that it has only two directions: forward or backward—up or down. Apparently there is no possibility that the American economy might cruise along at a moderate pace without piling on additional consumption. In fact, any cessation of economic growth will immediately start a downturn. "I cannot conceive a successful economy without growth," says Walter Heller, former Chairman of the President's Council of Economic Advisors,[3] and he is hardly alone.

Three strategies have been pursued in the United States ever since it was realized that consumption must be always on the increase. First, the government has increased its spending (and it has done so with deficit-building regularity). Second, an effort has been made to increase foreign sales of American products. Third, American consumers have been maneuvered into spending every dime they have, and even into spending future earnings by going into debt. It was as an aid to this third strategy that planned obsolescence was developed.

Vance Packard's book *The Waste Makers* is still the best and most comprehensive treatment of the systematic program of waste-making that characterizes the American economy. Having carefully studied the trade journals, the advertising campaigns, and the development of comprehensive marketing strategies, Packard is able to show that deliberate and calculated waste is a central ingredient of our economy.

As he defines it, planned obsolescence refers to a series of strategies with one end in mind: that a product, once sold to a customer, will be discarded as quickly as possible, to be replaced by the purchase of another. There are several ways to achieve this aim. First and foremost is product "death-dating." This simply means that the product is designed to fall apart or become unrepairable after a certain period of time. From a sales point of view, the ideal death date is just after the guarantee expires or as soon as the final installment is paid. This strategy, as we all know, has been applied to automobiles, appliances, furniture, and toys with great success.

Another strategy is to get consumers to use a product once, or relatively few times, and then throw it away. Plastic utensils, cups, and plates, paper towels, throwaway diapers—all are examples of a phenomenally wasteful area of production. And to this, of course, should be added the millions of tons of newspaper discarded every year and the 26 billion bottles, 48 billion metal cans, and 65 billion bottle caps discarded annually.[4]

Another major stategy is that of outmoding. Though the product recently purchased is still fully usable and functional, consumers are persuaded that it is hopelessly out-of-date. The most successful area for this strategy has, of course, been that of men's and women's clothing. Automobiles run a close second, and it is important to recognize that this same strategy has been applied to one industry after another throughout the economy. "New, improved" toothpaste or mouthwash or detergents or razor blades are all examples, as is the increasing tendency to come out with annual model changes in refrigerators, stoves, television sets, radios, and tape recorders. These changes add little or nothing to the usability of the product, but only tend to "outdate" former models in terms of looks—color coordination and the like—or unnecessary additional gadgetry.

A final strategy is to make things that are virtually unrepairable owing to design or prohibitive repair costs. Often the parts for repairs are simply not made available, or they are withdrawn from the market after a few years. This strategy has been used very successfully with automobiles, in which the cost of a standard repair (fixing a rumpled fender, for example) has continually escalated, and in which a point is soon reached where a car is virtually "falling apart" and costs more to keep in repair than to replace with a new one. It has also been used with electrical appliances, radio and television, children's toys, watches, and games and equipment.

It is important to realize that these strategies are deliberate and calculated. They are utilized in almost every sector of American industry and are tools that have been consciously developed to make sure that consumption keeps going, whatever the cost in resources, whatever the cost to the environment.

Here are some examples of the evolving strategy of planned obsolescence, as detailed by Vance Packard and others:

General Motors executive Floyd Allen, 1929: "Advertising is in the business of making people healthily dissatisfied with what they have in favor of something better. The old factors of wear and tear can no longer be depended upon to create a demand. They are too slow."[5]

Leon Kelly, in *Printer's Ink,* 1936: "It grows more and more apparent that the modern cycle of over-production and market glutting leaves practically no room for mankind's old, old ideas about long-lasting products. . . . Above all, we face the task of selling the whole public away from the deep-rooted idea of durability."[6]

Marketing consultant Victor Lebow, in *The Journal of Retailing* (mid-1950s): "Our enormous productive economy . . . demands that we make consumption our way of life, that we convert the buying and use of goods into rituals, that we seek our spiritual satisfactions, our ego satisfactions, in consumption. . . . We need things consumed, burned up, worn out, replaced, and discarded at an ever-increasing rate."[7]

Brooks Stevens, industrial designer (mid-1950s): "Our whole economy is based on planned obsolescence, and everybody who can read without moving his lips should know it by now. We make good products, we induce people to buy them, and then next year we deliberately introduce something that will make those products old-fashioned, out-of-date, obsolete. . . . It isn't organized waste. It's a sound contribution to the American economy."[8]

The automobile industry in America is an excellent case in

point for a more detailed examination of planned obsolescence. This industry plays a crucial role in maintaining the "good health" of our economic system. When it falters, this is taken as a bad omen for the entire economy; when it prospers, the financial pages rejoice. Since it employs, directly and indirectly, one out of seven workers in the United States this is hardly a surprise.

When General Motors executive Floyd Allen proclaimed in 1929 that "wear and tear" were just "too slow" to keep demand up, he must have been out of touch with the folks in the engineering department. Planned obsolescence was already a key market strategy of the automotive industry, so much so that just one year earlier it and the radio industry were being praised as "brilliant examples of what can be done with rapid obsolescence."[9]

The automobile industry has used every one of the obsolescence strategies I have outlined above. Cars are not built to be long-lasting, but quite the reverse. In 1960 the average trade-in time on an American car was two and one-fourth years and the average estimated life about ten years, or roughly half the expected life of a Volkswagen.[10] Chrome, trim, seat covers, and accessories are all expected to wear out rapidly and present a deteriorated look at just about the time the last payment is made on the car. Little effort has gone into making automobiles safer, more durable, or more economical. For example, Packard cites the following:

A major steel compay has had available for some time—with no takers—a lead-coated steel which, for *just 8 cents more* per auto muffler, would give a product that would last the life of the car. Instead, automakers are still installing mufflers that must be replaced on an average of once every two years at a cost to the consumer of $18 to $27 per muffler.[11]

In the 1920s Detroit began to pioneer the idea of the annual model change. This has meant that every year a new line of car models is offered to the public, each enthusiastically promoted as carrying the "latest" and "best" equipment, with the idea of persuading the consumers that their "old" jalopy is rapidly getting out-of-date. It is important to recognize that each annual model change adds to the production costs of the car. So, too, does the promotion of the new model. The advertising hoopla associated with the automotive industry was costing an estimated $200 per car in 1960.[12]

In 1962 the *Journal of Political Economy* reported on a pathbreaking study of the automobile industry by economists Franklin Fisher, Zvi Grilliches, and Carl Kaysen. These three researchers attempted to ascertain the cost to the consumer of the annual model change in the industry. Using the 1949 models as a base, they estimated that model changes, which were primarily cosmetic, were costing an average of $700 per car, or $3.9 billion per year over the 1956–1960 period. They also estimated that the decrease in fuel efficiency in the 1956–1960 period was costing drivers $1 billion a year.[13]

Economists Paul Baran and Paul Sweezy, in whose book *Monopoly Capital* this study is cited, took the inquiry one step further by asking themselves what would happen if the monopoly profits had been taken out, and if the best technology had been incorporated into production (the lead-coated steel muffler, for example). The cost of a well-designed car in 1960, they estimated, should have been around $700 to $800. "The total saving of resources would then be well above $11 billion a year. On this calculation, automobile model changes in the late 1950s were costing the country about 2.5 percent of its gross national product."[14]

With these strategies operating in the sale and production of automobiles, it is little wonder that each year Americans were junking seven million cars.[15] Imagine what those seven million cars represent in terms of steel, glass, aluminum, plastic—not to mention the power or the labor hours it took to make them or the cost of their disposal.

Other industries have been quick to follow the lead of the automobile manufacturers. The standard range for an average set of tires, for example, was 22,000 to 31,000 miles in 1954, but it had declined to a range of 18,000 to 27,000 just four years later.[16] In this same period, a Consumers' Union executive estimated that good wool rugs, which had once been made to last several generations, now had a lifespan of just ten years.[17] When General Electric had to go to court in 1941, a letter was brought to light in the trial which showed that the company had made a calculated decision to reduce the life-span of one of its bulbs from 1,000 to 750 hours.[18] In investigating the outdoor furniture industry, Vance Packard found that manufacturers were using aluminum only half as thick as that used a few years earlier. They were also using fewer strands in the webbing, and aluminum rivets instead of stainless-steel bolts. The net effect was that a standard chair was "easily destroyed by an adult over 140 pounds."[19]

In investigating the appliance industry, Packard's findings were much the same. Washers, dryers, refrigerators were all designed to fall apart and to need constant repair:

A part of the breakdown pattern apparently was the loading of appliances with gadgets that often immobilized the whole machine when they failed. Another aspect of the high breakage rates was the growing use of plastic parts that snapped or warped. . . . And then there were charges that appliance makers were cutting down on the gauge of steel, the size and number of bolts, and the quality of interior finishes where corrosion protection is important.[20]

To the waste caused by planned obsolescence should be added the costs of two related industries: advertising and packaging. After all, advertising's main purpose is to persuade people to buy, and early on the creative genius of Madison Avenue was turned to the task of convincing people that they needed the latest model in cars, or more fashionable clothes, or a color-coordinated bathroom. An estimated $20 billion a year was being spent on advertising in 1960—an expenditure of time and energy which would be virtually eliminated in any rationally designed economy.[21]

Product differentiation is another costly aspect of the advertising-consumption syndrome. Consumers must be lured into trying out and buying a host of virtually identical products; and to that end, brand names and ingenious packaging are employed. What is the use, for example, of there being 551 brands of coffee, 177 of salad dressing, and 249 of soap—each of them packaged differently, each of them huckstered in the market place?[22] In 1960 the cost of packaging was estimated at $25 billion, or roughly $500 per year per family in the United States. According to Al Fritsch of the Washington-based Center for Science in the Public Interest, most of this packaging is totally unnecessary. He estimates that for many products the packaging may have cost more than the actual contents and taken more energy to produce.

And apart from the obvious and awesome waste of the system of planned obsolescence there is the consideration of the human toll taken in the workers paid to keep this charade going. It makes little difference whether they are automobile workers, engineers, advertising people, or corporate executives. All have to live with the knowledge that they are perpetuating a system that is dishonest, environmentally destructive, wasteful, and geared to producing a systematically inferior product. What happens, then, to workers' self-respect, or sense that they are performing a socially useful function, or view of the meaning of life? In *Growing Up Absurd*, Paul Goodman gives a simple and pointed example:

Consider a likely useful job. A youth who is alert and willing but not "verbally intelligent"—perhaps he has quit high school at the eleventh grade (the median), as soon as he could—chooses for an auto mechanic. That's a good job, familiar to him, he often watched them as a kid. It's careful and dirty at the same time. In a small garage it's sociable; one can talk to the customers. . . . You please people by fixing their cars, and a man is proud to see rolling out on its own the car that limped in behind the tow truck. The pay is as good as the next fellow's who is respected.

So our young man takes this first-rate job. But what happens when he then learns that the cars have a built-in obsolescence, that the manufacturers do not want them to be repaired or repairable? They have lobbied a law that requires them to provide spare parts for only five years (it used to be ten). Repairing the new cars is often a matter of cosmetics, not mechanics; and the repairs are pointlessly expensive—a tail fin might cost $150. The insurance rates therefore double and treble on old and new cars both. Gone are the days of keeping the jalopies in good shape, the artist-work of a proud mechanic. But everybody is paying for foolishness, for in fact the new models are only trivially superior; the whole thing is a sell.

It is hard for the young man now to maintain his feelings of justification, sociability, serviceability. It is not surprising if he quickly becomes cynical and time-serving, interested in a fast buck. And so, on the notorious *Reader's*

Digest test, the investigators (coming in with a disconnected coil wire) found that 63 percent of mechanics charged for repairs they didn't make.[23]

Bad Technology

A second area of significant and environmentally detrimental waste in the American economy is found in the host of new technologies that have been adopted since World War II. In his book *The Closing Circle,* Barry Commoner shows that much of the spectacular rise in air and water pollution is due to the introduction of new technologies whose ecological impact was never considered.

For example, the replacement of soap by detergents in the American household has meant a twentyfold increase in the impact of phosphate on the environment, with a negligible increase in cleaning power.[24] Wool and cotton—two natural products that have made up the bulk of clothing production in the United States—are rapidly being replaced by synthetic fibers. These synthetic fibers (nylon, rayon, orlon, etc.) are produced petrochemically, and thus consume fuel stocks. They also require industrial processes that utilize enormous heat and cause a much greater incidence of air pollution.[25] Aluminum, which is replacing steel and lumber as a building material, requires fifteen times more fuel-energy consumption for its production than does steel and 150 times more than lumber. An aluminum beer can accounts for 6.3 times the energy consumption of a steel can.[26]

Truck transportation of goods, which—thanks to the highway lobby—has been given special advantages to compete with rail transport, is far more costly in environmental terms. "The energy required to move one ton of freight one mile by rail now averages about 624 btu (British thermal units), while trucks require about 3,460 btu per ton-mile. This means that, *for the same freight haulage,* trucks burn nearly six times as much fuel as railroads—and emit about six times as much environmental pollution. At the same time, the amount of power required to produce the cement and steel needed to lay down a mile of four-lane highway (essential for truck traffic) is 3.6

times the power needed to produce the steel track for comparable rail traffic. Finally, the highway takes up a 400-foot right of way, while the railroad takes only 100 feet."[27]

What becomes clear from Dr. Commoner's book is that the environmental crisis that has shaken us in recent years is to a great extent due to faulty and dangerous, *and largely unnecessary,* changes in our methods of production:

The statistical fiction, the "average American," now consumes, each year, about as many calories, protein, and other foods (although somewhat less of vitamins); uses about the same amount of clothes and cleaners; occupies about the same amount of newly constructed housing; requires about as much freight; and drinks about the same amount of beer (twenty-six gallons per capita!) as he did in 1946. However, his food is now grown on less land with more fertilizers and pesticides than before; his clothes are more likely to be made of synthetic fibers than of cotton or wool; he launders with synthetic detergent rather than soap; he lives and works in buildings that depend more heavily on aluminum and concrete and plastic, than on steel and lumber; the goods he uses are increasingly shipped by truck rather than rail; he drinks beer out of nonreturnable bottles or cans. . . . He is more likely to live in air-conditioned surroundings than before. He also drives about twice as far as he did in 1946, in a heavier car, on synthetic rather than natural rubber tires, using more gasoline per mile, . . . fed into an engine of increased horsepower and compression ratio.

This pattern of economic growth is the major reason for the environmental crisis. A good deal of the mystery and confusion about the sudden emergence of the environmental crisis can be removed by pinpointing, pollutant by pollutant, how the post-war technological transformation of the United States economy has produced not only the much heralded 126 percent rise in Gross National Product but also, *at a rate about ten times faster than the growth of the Gross National Product,* the rising levels of environmental pollution [italics added].[28]

Dr. Commoner estimates that about half the productive plant investment since World War II, or $600 billion's worth, has been based on this faulty technology. And that rather awesome figure, he reckons, is what it would cost to put our industrial system on a sound environmental footing. Giving ourselves twenty-five years to make the changeover, this represents an annual investment of some $40 billion.[29] Of course, this assessment is based on the assumption that we would continue to consume at our current level. It does not consider the possibility of a simplified production system, nor does it consider what our needs would be if we were producing durable and solid goods. Nevertheless it does give some idea of just how far our economy has sunk into ecologically dangerous production and provides a measure of just how extensive and drastic a change would be in order if we set about the process of redesign.

Wasted Talent

A final anomaly in the American economy concerns the way we use the creative talents of our people. We are a country possessing enormous wealth in what some consider to be the most precious commodity today: education. We are almost universally literate; we have the greatest number of college graduates in the world; we have libraries, computers, universities, and think-tanks. And yet most of our brain power is going to waste. It is devoted to producing and selling inferior goods, or administering poorly designed educational and welfare systems, or thinking up new ways to kill our fellow human beings.

In his book *Design for the Real World,* Victor Papanek decries this terrible waste of talent:

Before (in the "good old days"), if a person liked killing people, he had to become a general, purchase a coal mine, or else study nuclear physics. Today, industrial design has put murder on a mass production basis. By designing criminally unsafe automobiles that kill or maim nearly one million people around the world each year, by creating whole new series of permanent garbage to clutter up the landscape, and by choosing materials and processes that pollute the air we breathe, designers have become a dangerous breed.[30]

Papenek estimates that $20 billion is set aside each year for research and design, and that 90 percent of that money is used to finance projects that make no real contribution to our people or to the world.[31] He suggests hundreds of areas where design research could make a significant contribution to human needs—for example, in improving product safety, in developing items for the use of the handicapped and illiterate, in discovering methods of storing food more efficiently in developing countries. Designers could be spending time usefully in working out simple and ecological transportation systems for both developed and developing lands, or planning for paramedical health equipment, or environmentally sound mass housing, or machinery that can be used in villages to build homes or pump water. Creative talent is needed in developing new energy sources, new methods of agricultural technology, and adaptable communications equipment for varied cultures.

Papanek and his students try to use their talent for such purposes, and thus far have developed a nine-cent single-band radio that operates on cow dung, a six-dollar refrigerator for tropical use, and an eight-dollar television set that would be ideal for village educational distribution. They have also developed a new system for seeding and reclaiming desert land, a thermometer for illiterates, and a pump that can be made from discarded tires. The ingenuity represented by their small-scale efforts gives a faint glimmering of what could be accomplished through the employment of numbers of people in socially useful industrial designing.

One of Papanek's students has developed a rather remarkable means of personal transportation: an electrically powered scooter built from aluminum that folds up to the size of a shoebox and weighs just 18 pounds. It has a cruising range of 15 miles, takes up only 9 x 15 inches of road space, and is in general ideal for inner-city travel. The student worked for seven months and expended $425 to develop his miniscooter. His former instructor points out that in the same year General Motors spent $3.4 billion on "research and design," supposedly to meet the nation's transportation needs.[32]

It is difficult to calculate the probable cost to the nation and the world of our appalling waste of creative and talented people. The toll taken by poor and faulty design alone is staggering: 50,000 killed and 600,000 injured in the United States each year in auto accidents; 700,000 children injured by unsafe toys; 250,000 injured by unsafe home appliances; and, according to the National Heart Association, five years taken off the lives of 50 percent of America's workers owing to the stress occasioned by noisy equipment.[33] And this is only the tip of the iceberg. What of all the lives that could have been saved by better food-production technology? Or by controlling pollution before it got out-of-hand? Or by greater attention to basic health technology and to literacy programs in developing countries? Or by devising alternatives to the world's urban slums? And what if the best talents had been hard at work throughout this century designing alternatives to war, or a more equitable international production and distribution system?

The possibilities are endless, and in that realization lies a measure of genuine hope.

DESIGN PROBLEMS IN THE THIRD WORLD

Our third area of investigation into the major global design problems is concerned with the development strategies of the noncommunist Third World countries. With the dissolution of colonial rule in Africa, the Middle East, and Asia a host of new countries found themselves faced with the urgent question of economic development to meet the needs of their people. The leaders of most countries chose to follow a path of development that linked their national economy with the international capitalist market economy—that is, with the trade and exchange system dominated by the United States and Europe (and later, Japan).

It would hardly be accurate to say that the people of these nations chose such an affiliation, since in most instances they were not consulted. Had they been consulted, it is unlikely that they would have understood the implications of the choice. What happened in most instances was that the national leadership, itself primarily composed of the merchants, business people, landowners, who were profiting from the present system (most of them educated in Western-oriented schools and universities), simply chose to remain within the sphere of Western economic influence and trade arrangements.

When such countries approached the question of development, they were presented with a model that aped the supposed history of economic development in the industrial countries. The important thing, it was thought, was to boost the gross national product by developing an industrial base. This could supposedly be done by allowing investments for industrial production to come in from the outside, by creating an industrially supportive infrastructure (highways, docking facilities, airports, hydroelectric plants), and by concentrating on the sale of raw materials and other products abroad in order to bring in the foreign exchange that would be needed for the purchase of technical equipment. Such a process, it was thought, would help to develop a strong and capable middle class of managers and administrators, plus a reasonably skilled pool of industrial workers. The end goal of this process was to arrive one day at a national economy which was a model in miniature of that of the United States, or France, or Great Britain.

The results of this development design have not been good. Attention to the industrial sector has most often meant a lack of interest and investment in the agricultural sector—and it is in the rural areas and villages that most of the world's people subsist. Instead of investment in rural education agricultural improvement, basic health and sanitation, and small-scale, village-based manufacturing, most countries concentrated on road and airport construction, investment in heavy industry, the production of "cash crops" like tea and coffee, and the educational needs of their elite.

Dr. E. F. Schumacher, the Britain-based planner who for years has made the development needs of the Third World his business, gives a picture of what this pattern has meant:

A textile mill I visited in Africa provides a telling example. The manager showed me with considerable pride that his factory was at the highest technological level to be found anywhere in the world. Why was it so highly automated? "Because," he said, "African labour, unused to industrial work, would make mistakes, whereas automated machinery does not make mistakes. The quality standards demanded today," he explained, "are such that my product must be perfect in order to find a market."

. . . Nor is this all. Because of inappropriate quality standards, all his equipment had to be imported from the most advanced countries; the sophisticated equipment demanded that all higher management and maintenance personnel had to be imported. Even the raw materials had to be imported because the locally grown cotton was too short for top quality yarn and the postulated standards demanded the use of a high percentage of manmade fibers.

This is not an untypical case. Anyone who has taken the trouble to look systematically at actual "development" projects—instead of merely studying development plans and econometric models—knows of countless such cases: soap factories producing such luxury soap by such sensitive processes that only highly refined materials can be used, which must be imported at high prices while the local raw materials are exported at low prices; food-processing plants; packing stations; motorisation, and so on.[34]

Examples of the distortions of this system are myriad: the shiny hotels and office buildings that go up in the capital cities while thousands and hundreds of thousands of people live in mud huts or cardboard shacks; expenditures to build automobile construction plants while the vast bulk of the populace lack the rudiments of a drinkable water supply; the shrimp that is caught off the coast of Mexico and shipped to the United States, while inland people are diseased from lack of protein; the fish that is canned in Morocco, and goes to feed European pets rather than hungry people in North Africa.

The emphasis on industrialization on the large-scale model, and for the international market, has meant that millions of dollars and thousands of labor hours are being wasted on the production of goods and services that contribute almost nothing to the basic needs of these countries' people. It was supposed that the money earned by such enterprises would be used to purchase local products or invested in other enterprises that would provide jobs. What has happened instead is that the local elites, who own the factories or reap some of their profits, choose to spend their money on luxury items from abroad, convert it into gold, or salt it away in Swiss bank accounts. The system of Western-style industrialization and private enterprise has resulted in a lopsided economy that easily meets the needs of the national elite but almost completely bypasses those of the mass of people.

In the rural sectors, where the lack of gainful employment and of the necessities of life is a perennial problem, people decide in desperation to migrate to the cities, hoping that there perhaps they can find a job, or work a pedicab, or beg in the streets. Since few jobs are available, Third World urban centers soon find themselves surrounded by massive slums whose destitute populations are on the edge of existence. These people have been driven there by the "development" policies of their leaders—policies which, it should be noted, have been promoted and encouraged by the large capitalist countries. For these countries' interest lies in providing the large capital equipment, the cars, and the technology that go with this model, and in purchasing the tea and pet food that come to them at cut-rate prices.

Since most of us have been raised on this model of growth and development, it is often hard to imagine what another model might look like. Ivan Illich, an educator who has worked closely with Latin American development, has provided an example that may help to "shake loose" our thinking.

Imagine, he says, that instead of spending $100 million to construct a concrete highway between two points in some underdeveloped country, developers spent it to cut a latticework of small trails between villages which could be traversed by "mechanical donkeys," traveling five miles per hour and capable of carrying loads of a ton or more. If fifty thousand miles of these trails could be cut between thousands of villages, and if enough simple land-cruising vehicles were provided, what might be the result in establishing a trade and exchange infrastructure between these now isolated villages? Would it not, he asks, mean the creation of a linking system that would encourage communication, increase trade and the manufacture of village crafts for internal use, and generally take an entire population one step forward in self-sufficiency and development?

To Illich the pattern of development that has been pursued by most Latin American countries, with the aid and encouragement of the United States (and the active discouragement of any other model—e.g., our actions with regard to Chile, Guatemala, and Cuba), borders on the criminal:

Traffic jams develop in São Paulo while almost a million Northeastern Brazilians flee the drought by walking 500 miles. Each car which Brazil puts on the road denies fifty people good transportation by bus. Every dollar spent in Latin America on doctors and hospitals costs a hundred lives. . . . Had each dollar been spent on providing safe drinking water, a hundred lives could have been saved.[35]

There is much more that could be said about this pattern of development. My purpose here is not to be exhaustive, but simply to point to another area in which system redesign could contribute mightily to the welfare of the world and its people.

CONCLUSION

I have attempted in this chapter to consider in some detail three areas of poor design in our present global system. There are other areas I could have considered—the global food production and distribution system, for example, or world patterns of energy use and production—but these three should suffice to make my point: namely, that the present world system of resource use contains major flaws and discontinuities that should be corrected by redesign to provide for the needs of all the people.

In a later chapter I will take up the question of how our system might be reorganized and what some of the principles of that reorganization might be. First, however, I would like to turn to a further consideration of the workings of the system, looking specifically at the place of the United States economy in a global perspective. From there I will turn to a discussion of the impact of all this information on the minds of people in the affluent countries and of how we ourselves can begin to respond to it.

NOTES

1. Quoted in Vance Packard, *The Waste Makers* (New York: McKay, 1960), p. 102.
2. Ibid., p. 17.
3. Quoted in E.F. Schumacher, *Small Is Beautiful* (New York: Harper, 1973), p. 112.
4. John V. Taylor, *Enough Is Enough* (London: SCM Press, 1975), p. 27.
5. *Printer's Ink,* October 10, 1929; quoted in Harvey Salgo, "The Obsolescence of Growth: Capitalism and the Environmental Crisis," in *The Review of Radical Political Economics,* vol. 5, no. 3 (Fall 1973), p. 31.
6. Ibid.
7. Quoted in Packard, *The Waste Makers,* p. 24.
8. Ibid., p. 54.
9. Quoted in Salgo, "The Obsolescence of Growth," p. 31.
10. Packard, *The Waste Makers,* p. 24.
11. Ibid., p. 99.
12. Ibid., p. 88.
13. Cited in Paul Baran and Paul Sweezy, *Monopoly Capital* (New York: Modern Reader, 1966).
14. Ibid., p. 137.
15. Taylor, *Enough Is Enough,* p. 27.
16. Packard, *The Waste Makers,* p. 98.
17. Ibid., p. 112.
18. Salgo, "The Obsolescence of Growth," p. 32.
19. *The Waste Makers,* p. 116.
20. Ibid., p. 104.
21. Baran and Sweezy, *Monopoly Capital,* p. 119.
22. Packard, *The Waste Makers,* p. 228.
23. New York: Random, 1956, pp. 19–20.
24. Barry Commoner, *The Closing Circle* (New York: Bantam, 1972), p. 156.
25. Ibid., p. 158.
26. Ibid, pp. 170–71.
27. Ibid., pp. 169–70.
28. Ibid., pp. 143–44.
29. Ibid., p. 284.
30. New York: Bantam, 1973, p. 329.
31. Ibid., p. 109.
32. Ibid., p. 248.
33. Ibid., p. 99.
34. *Small Is Beautiful,* p. 184.
35. Taylor, *Enough Is Enough,* p. 98.

3. Rich World, Poor World?

Our picture of the global situation would not be complete, or even accurate, without a closer look at the interworkings of the international production and distribution system.

THE POVERTY OF THE THIRD WORLD

First, it should be observed that much of the "poor" world is not poor at all. As the successful oil producers' cartel has shown (and rumors of similar struggles over Third World riches in copper, tin, bauxite, and cocoa abound), the very significant fact is that First World affluence depends in large part on Third World resources. It is estimated that the United States already imports 40 percent of its raw materials from abroad and that most of this comes from underdeveloped countries.[1] A survey made in the early 1960s revealed that the advanced industrial nations relied on the Third World for 93 percent of their crude oil, 76 percent of their rubber, 49 percent of their raw lumber, 86 percent of their tin, 88 percent of their bauxite (for aluminum production), and so on.[2]

India, considered poor on everyone's list, has about 23 percent of the world's known iron reserves, and Latin America has "vast reserves of oil, iron, copper, tin, gold, zinc, lead: the list is endless."[3]

But if the Third World, or at least large segments of it, is rich, why are its people so poor? Is it, as some surmise, because they are lazy? Or because they have too many babies? Or because they lack the expertise, and perhaps the interest, in greater development? The answer to such speculations has to be no. Third World people lead lives of toil. The struggle for subsistence is the daily concern of the poor throughout the world; they require all the energy they have just to keep alive.

Nor can the population growth rate be adduced in many Third World countries as the primary cause of poverty or the greatest obstacle to successful development. As China has shown, a nation with sufficient motivation and vision can mobilize its vast army of potential laborers in a concerted effort for across-the-board development. And as material conditions improve and food, health care, and old-age security are provided for, the process has as one of its side effects the motivation to have smaller families and to plan for the future.[4]

With regard to the question of expertise, it must be conceded that there is a great need for trained people in the health, agricultural, industrial, and economic sectors. Motivation, however, is not lacking: People everywhere are interested in improving their material situation if only they can be shown a better way to do so. Many of the stories about lazy workers, change-resistant farmers, and uninterested villagers have arisen because the development planners themselves did not understand the cultural and economic structures of the areas they were attempting to change. As cooperative projects in the Dominican Republic, in Panama, Cuba, China, and India have shown, it is not hard to engage people in the process of development once they are truly convinced that the project will result in some tangible benefit to themselves or their families.

For a more accurate picture of why development has not succeeded in the nonsocialist countries of the Third World, it is necessary to return to the setting of two of our earlier examples of life in the underdeveloped lands.

Readers will recall Allah Dad, the Pakistani who cuts grass

seven days a week for his family's buffalo. In the *New York
Times* series that portrayed Mr. Dad's life, reporter James
Sterba gave a simple but significant glimpse into the system
that keeps Mr. Dad, and a fellow worker named Sanab Gul,
locked into their poverty:

> When Mr. Dad, 43 years old, and Mr. Gul, 50, stand to stretch the stiffness
> from their legs, they can see the expensive painted residences and buildings
> of Islamabad, Pakistan's decade-old national capital, where government
> workers live and where goats and sheep are prohibited from grazing. They
> can see large expensive cars, carrying men wearing suits and ties, going by
> on paved roads.
>
> For years after Field Marshall Mohammed Ayub Khan assumed military
> power in 1958 and imposed the political stability favorable for aid loans and
> foreign investment, Pakistan was cited as a model worthy of emulation.
> Agricultural production jumped, roads were paved, cities blossomed.
>
> However, the new wealth was concentrated in few hands. A small group
> of energetic businessmen, known as the 22 families, have long controlled
> more than 80 percent of the wealth.[5]

Pakistan, in other words, tried the "Western" road to development, complete with foreign aid and technical assistance
from the United States and other rich countries and encouragement of outside investments in the exploitation of national
resources. The net result of this approach was that a few
Pakistanis got richer, while the mass of people stayed the
same, or saw their condition get worse. For example, the
government of Pakistan conceded at the end of the 1960s that,
while the economy had witnessed a healthy growth rate, unemployment had increased and real wages in the industrial
sector had declined by up to one-third.[6] An examination of
the effects of the "green revolution" (the planned introduction of new, high-yielding seeds and new crop methods) in the
Pakistani countryside found that the income of landless
laborers had not changed in five years. On the other hand,
one landlord who held 1,500 acres of wheat land conceded to
the researchers that he had cleared a $100,000 profit on his
operations in the previous year.[7]

The situation in Indonesia is much the same. Pitung, our

pedicab driver and trash picker, literally lives on the other side of the tracks from a world very different from his own. Within sight of his cardboard shack,

> foreign businessmen pay $800 a month or more for renovated, air-conditioned houses with manicured front gardens and varnished bamboo fences. Other houses facing the tracks are occupied by army officers, local businessmen, and ranking civil servants.
>
> Here, within the space of half a football field, are two worlds. One is the world of wide streets built for people who have cars to drive on them, office buildings with elevators that people ride for transportation rather than adventure. There are taxis, hotels, restaurants and nightclubs for the people who can afford them, and telephones for people who know someone they can call.
>
> Unfortunately, only about 20 percent of the nearly five million residents of Jakarta live in this section of town. It is the other world that the remaining 80 percent live as Mr. Pitung lives—a little better or a little worse.[8]

The story of development in Indonesia is much the same as in Pakistan—a military coup in 1966, followed by a Western-oriented development policy that encouraged outside investment. Statistically, the results have been good: foreign exchange reserves have gone from a deficit to a billion-dollar surplus; oil revenues are $4 billion a year; gross national product is up; construction of office buildings and roads is up. But as one local newspaper conceded, "the lot of the common people has not changed at all." The average Indonesian subsists on 1,600 calories a day (half the United States intake), 54 percent of the population are illiterate, and 60 percent live in shacks.[9]

Wherever one looks in the so-called free world (or that sector of the Third World which is in the international capitalist market economy), the picture is much the same. In Brazil, which United States newspapers single out as a production "dynamo" and economic " "miracle," twelve years of development at a 10 percent annual increase have resulted in the betterment of only 5 percent of the people; the living standard of 45 percent became worse and that of the remaining 50 percent stayed the same.[10] In Mexico, the home of the "Green Revolution," it was discovered that 80 percent of the agricultural growth since 1950 could be directly attributed to the top 3 percent of farmers and that during that period the number of days worked by a landless laborer declined from 194 to 100, owing to increased mechanization. Real wages for these workers dropped from $68 to $56 a year.[11]

As a final example, we cite the conclusion of the *New York Times* team that surveyed the economic conditions of Asia and the Pacific:

For rich Asians—and for a small but growing middle class in a number of countries— . . . economic growth has provided more goods to buy, more food to eat, more comfort and more luxury.

But probably the majority of Asians still share little of this growth. In fact, not only is the gap between the poor nations of Asia and the rich industrialized nations still widening, but the gap between rich and poor within the poor countries is widening.

The Asian poor do not yet have the cars and television sets produced by industrialized society. But they do have the new problems of an affluent society: air and water pollution, traffic jams, chaotic flows of population from the countryside into the cities, mushrooming slums, technological unemployment and breakdown of government services.[12]

What these examples and surveys point out is that the pattern of development that ties underdeveloped countries to the investment patterns and market enterprises of the rich countries has had little or no impact on the bulk of the poor. What has happened instead is that a handful of local bankers, business people, and government and military employees has had its material condition improved while the rest of the populace has been left to fend for itself. The simple fact is that this national elite is "on the take" from rich-world corporations and governments and is concerned primarily with its own favored position. No wonder, then, that World Bank President Robert MacNamara, when considering the plight of the "hundreds of millions of desperately poor people throughout the whole of the developing world," should conclude that "development is simply not reaching them in any degree."[13]

The problem, however, is not that the underdeveloped lands happen to be unfortunate in lacking enlightened leaders who take the masses' interests to heart. The problem is, on the contrary, that selfish national elite are encouraged, supported, and maintained in power by covert and overt actions of rich-world corporations and governments. They are maintained because, so long as they get their share, they are willing to subordinate their countries' economies to the resource needs and investment interest of the rich and powerful countries.

Again, an examination of United States policy and practice will serve to illustrate these points.

THE UNITED STATES AND THE THIRD WORLD*

The United States has a very real strategic interest in maintaining the flow of Third World resources to its shores. As the recent oil crisis showed, our economy is vulnerable to the restriction of raw materials. As noted above, we now import over 40 percent of our materials used in production, and the indications are that in the future we shall need even more. As far back as 1954 American policy makers were keenly aware that continued United States economic well-being was dependent on foreign resources. In that year a special commission reported to the President that

from the viewpoint of our long-term economic growth and the viewpoint of our national defense, the shift of the United States from the position of a net exporter of metals and minerals to that of a net importer is of overshadowing significance in shaping our foreign economic policies.

We have always been almost entirely dependent on imports for tin, nickel, and the platinum group of metals. In addition, our requirements for asbestos, chromite, graphite, manganese, mercury, mica, and tungsten have been generally covered by imports. . . . At present, by contrast, the United States is fully self-sufficient only in coal, sulfur, potash, molybdenum, and magnesium.[14]

National security planners have often observed that a safe

---

*Special thanks are due to William Moyer, who gathered much of the information cited in the following pages. For a more extensive discussion of these questions, see his chapter "The Exported Plague" in *Moving Toward a New Society*, Susanne Gowan et al., available from New Society Press, 4722 Baltimore Avenue, Philadelphia, Pennsylvania 19143 ($3.68 post paid).

and assured supply of needed raw materials is a crucial factor in military defense, and the United States has therefore a strong strategic interest in seeing to it that the leadership of resource-exporting countries is sympathetic to American interests. Nor is United States political leadership unmindful of the fact that the economy as well is dependent on a regular and increasing flow of raw materials. Thus, in a government publication on natural resources, a former secretary of the interior issues this warning: "The extent to which a nation possesses or controls natural resources is probably the most important determinant of its world position. We will disregard this principle at our peril."[15]

In addition to the political and military considerations of our national government, United States-based corporations have a vital interest in the continued flow of Third World resources. After all, such materials are needed for the manufacture and processing of many of the goods which go onto the market. Many American industries such as those engaged in aircraft and aluminum production simply could not function without the constant inflow of resources from abroad.

A second interest of United States corporations in Third World resources is the very high profits to be made from investment in their extraction and sale. Since World War II the return on investments in the developing countries has been double what a similar investment would be in a developed economy. That being the case, it is understandable that United States and European corporations have vied with each other, avid for a cut of the take. Between 1950 and 1965 United States corporations took $25.8 billion in profits from Third World enterprises.[16] A sizeable 13 percent of all United States corporate profits are estimated to be generated by holdings in the developing lands.[17]

And that is not all. Many corporations do not "repatriate" their foreign profits back to the United States, but instead use them to invest in other foreign ventures. Thus the president of General Motors was able to report to his stockholders that General Motors' net capital and fixed assets overseas had grown from $180 million in 1950 to $1.1 billion in 1965 and that virtually all of this growth had occurred without additional investment from the home office.[18]

Since it is no secret that United States corporations have significant influence in the setting of both domestic and foreign policy, it can safely be said that American policy with regard to foreign leadership is decidedly biased in favor of those national figures who (1) will encourage or permit foreign investment, (2) can be regarded as friendly to the United States and its strategic interests, and (3) can be counted on to protect United States property and corporate holdings.

To ensure a favorable attitude on the part of the Third World governments toward our "interests," the United States is possessed of a number of tools for exercising its influence.

The first is in the area of *trade*. The exchange of goods between nations has long been a feature of human civilization. Since world resources are not evenly distributed, and since some societies develop techniques and abilities before others, it is only natural that extensive trade should develop around the globe. In the modern international economy, trade becomes a factor in the functioning of every society. Developed countries are interested in trade because they need a flow of raw materials for their factories, want manufactured goods from other industrial countries, or desire to obtain goods not easily produced on their own soil.

Thus the United States brings in bauxite from Jamaica, coffee from Brazil, bananas from Honduras, oil from the Middle East, cameras from Germany, and so on. These countries in turn may be interested in purchasing tractors, computers, petroleum refinery equipment, soybeans, wheat, communications equipment, and airplanes. Participation in the game of trade requires that a country possess a certain reserve of claims on foreign currencies, or gold, so that it can back up the international purchasing power of its currency. The way a country accumulates these "foreign reserves" is through exporting its goods. Thus even revolutionary China allows the continued craft of jade work—though it is meant for the capitalist luxury market—in order to earn some of the foreign credits it needs to purchase outside goods.

To be denied access to the normal channels of trade, then, is to find your country in a decidedly difficult position. This Fidel Castro discovered when the United States moved to "blockade" his economy after he had seized the property of certain American corporations. The American blockade meant that Cuba did not have access to the medical equipment, motor vehicle repair parts, wheat, and other products it had traditionally obtained from the United States. It also meant that the lucrative American market for Cuban sugar was cut off. In a recent interview, the Cuban premier described this blockade as "cruel" and said that it had severely hampered the pace of development in his country.

However, a total blockade of trade is a tool not normally resorted to. Often it is sufficient to threaten a restriction of trade on one or two crucial commodities. For example, the United States has recently been in conflict with Japan over the issue of the supposed "dumping" of cheap shoes, textiles, and small electric goods on the American market. Such low-cost selling, American manufacturers claimed, was undercutting domestic sales and threatening to bankrupt companies, leave American workers jobless, and so on. When United States policy makers proceeded to talk publicly about possible import quotas or tariffs on Japanese goods, a bilateral conference quickly ensued and an informal agreement was reached that purportedly satisfied all parties.

If a threat of United States trade restrictions is enough to bring a major industrial power to heel, imagine the power of a similar threat to a developing country which may depend on the sale of only one or two commodities for its foreign earnings.

In fact, the ideal workings of international trade—which would appear to be so mutually beneficial to all parties—are rarely experienced by the developing countries. One major problem is that the already industrialized countries maintain extensive tariff walls against the importation of certain goods into their national markets. This is usually done to protect their own industries from outside competition. Thus India may be able to export unlimited raw cotton to England but be restricted in the quantity of finished textiles it can sell in that country. Brazil may be able to send its coffee beans to the United States, but not instant coffee already bottled. Argentina may be able to send leather to North America, but not shoes. This practice, of course, means that the further industrial expansion of Third World economies is seriously hampered. The logical result of such policies is to keep the developing countries in a permanent condition of underdevelopment, restricting their role to that of supplying raw materials which we, in turn, process and then sell back to them in the form of finished goods.

Another part of the picture is that developing countries, already restricted in the areas in which they can earn foreign currency, find themselves forced to turn to the production of goods and services that are permitted by the developed countries. Thus valuable crop land may be switched from the production of foodstuff to the production of tea for foreign markets, or a government may find itself occupied with building a new airport and roads to the central city (not to mention hotels, swimming pools, bars, restaurants, and nightclubs) in order to attract and hold the tourist trade.

Some developmental economists have argued that the very participation of developing countries in the international market economy is detrimental to their authentic development. They point out that Mexico sends 90 percent of its shrimp catch to the United States because Americans are willing to pay good prices for it. Yet that same amount of shrimp, if consumed in protein-short Mexico, would increase the average protein intake of each and every Mexican by 25 percent.[19] Similarly, the anchovy catch off the coast of Peru, if consumed in South America rather than being sent as cattle feed to the United States and Europe, would raise the dietary level of South Americans to that of Southern Europe.[20]

It is argued that if developing countries concentrated on their internal development and on producing and manufacturing as much as they possibly could by themselves without relying on their tourism or bananas or cocoa to buy outside goods, there is the possibility that such countries would develop strong, self-sufficient economies. Where a country is too small or too lacking in needed resources, it is encouraged to consider participation in a regional development program. Essentially, this has been the development strategy of the People's Republic of China. The African country of Tanzania is also trying a similar experiment.

A second area of considerable influence is in *investment*. Traditionally, the attraction of foreign investment in the extraction of resources or production of agricultural goods has been regarded as a favorable addition to a country's development. This is understandable, since many Third World countries have not had the capital, the technology, the trained workers, or the international market connections to develop their own resources for the international market. Therefore, it has seemed attractive and sensible to allow foreign-based companies to come in, erect factories, dig mines, and establish plantations, when the alternative would seem to be leaving these resources untouched and the perpetuation of a chronic "backward" economy. After all, such operations generate tax revenues for the host country; they employ local labor, and their imported employees spend part of their salaries in the locale; and there may even be some provision for profit-sharing between the investor and the government or between the investor and a group of local investors. In addition to such altruistic motives, many local politicians are influenced to favor foreign investment through direct or indirect bribery. A personal cut of the take, places on the payroll for one's family, or a direct under-the-table gift—those are all tried and true methods for economic penetration into new economies, and are most often accepted as a normal part of business dealings abroad (and, it seems, as a part of domestic business dealings as well).

The extent of such investments in Third World countries is astonishing. In 1970, for example, *Newsweek* magazine reported that United States investors employed two million South Americans, paid one-fifth of all taxes in South America, and produced one-third of all its exports.[21] And this is the record only of United States investment; it does not include investment from Western Europe, Japan, and Canada.

The extent of foreign involvement in Third World economies is enormous. Thus Brazil, the economic giant of South America, has a stunning eighty-two percent of its industry held in American hands.[22] And in Peru, where American investment is very high, and which is considered to be "not atypical" in its degree of foreign ownership, the following description (circa 1970) has been made:

Anderson Clayton dominates the wool and cotton production market. The Grace Co., the Chase Manhattan Bank, the First National City Bank of New York, the Northern Peru Mines, Marcona Mines, and Goodyear establish the prices for agricultural products and control 80 percent of the raw materials. The International Petroleum Company (IPC), a subsidiary of Standard of New Jersey, owns the oil that represents 80 percent of the national production. The American Smelting and Refining Company and Cerro de Pasco Corp., which owns over 1.2 million acres, reign over copper and other mining production. The Bell Telephone Co. has taken over the telephone services. . . . [23]

There are several problems presented by such deep foreign involvement in Third World countries. First of all, the effective control of the country's resources passes from its hands into those of foreign investors. While it may appear that the government of a country is determining the rate and nature of its resource exploitation, this is in fact being done by the companies that employ so many people, pay such a large proportion of the taxes, and have in effect bought so many local friends in the legislature, the executive branch, and the military. Companies threatened by local governments can often do what many companies do right here in the United States in the face of proposed legislation they regard as unfavorable—threaten to leave or to curtail operations. Often such procedures would mean a marked reduction in tax revenues, local unemployment, a loss of foreign currency, and a general downturn in the economy.

A second and related problem is that foreign investors put their money into production that will earn them a profit, and most often such enterprises are not the optimal way in which resources or labor power could be used. For example, a foreign automobile company may decide that a plant to produce automobile frames should be located in, say, Brazil. The frames may then be shipped to another Latin American country where the rest of the car is assembled. Optimal resource planning for Brazil, however, may indicate that the steel and labor power which is going into this enterprise would be better used to develop tractors and agricultural machinery for domestic use. Unless Brazil can convince the foreign investor that such a transfer is profitable, or unless the government has sufficient power to force a bargain, this misuse of resources will go on unchecked.

What emerges from this investment pattern is that Third World countries often end up in the position of producing goods of no great value to their people, and producing them in a piecemeal approach that does not significantly increase the possibility of domestic self-reliance or balanced industrial development.

The third problem with foreign investment is that after an initial period when new money is flowing in, the situation reverses itself and the underdeveloped countries find themselves becoming net losers in the economic process. For example, in 1967 Latin America sent back $1 billion more in profits than it had coming in from United States investment. In 1970 United States investors got back $4.9 billion more than they invested in Third World countries;[24] and in the fifteen-year period between 1950 and 1965, American investors received $25.8 billion from the Third World while they sent only $9 billion in new investments.[25] At the same time, United States and other investors were able to use some of their local profits to purchase other enterprises and launch new programs in the Third World, thus increasing their hold on resources.

What this might mean in terms of the development of a country's economy can best be illustrated by examination of a case study. In a book on United States influence abroad, ominously entitled *The Enemy*, Felix Greene considers the example of the Cyprus Mines Corporation. An American owned corporation that held two large copper mines in Cyprus, it operated as that country's largest employer from 1912 until the early 1960s. The company prided itself on its enlightened local policies; and thus it paid higher than average wages and put some millions of its dollars into housing for its employees, schools, hospitals, food-supplement programs, and so on. At the same time, it repatriated over $100 million in profits to its stockholders in the United States. Some of this $100 million was used philanthropically, to establish Harvey Mudd College (named after the company's president) in Claremont, California, and to endow buildings at the University of Southern California and Columbia University. But the bulk of the profits were reinvested, and thus the company added to its portfolio an iron mine in Peru, a copper mine in Arizona, a shipping company in Panama, a cement plant in Hawaii, two chemical plants in the Netherlands, and an iron mine in Australia.

Meanwhile, back in Cyprus, the mines became exhausted; the employees were dismissed, the food program was ended, and Cyprus was left with almost nothing to show for this irretrievable loss of resources.

As the American socialist magazine the *Monthly Review* commented:

Imagine where Cyprus could be today if it had been able to borrow the capital to exploit [the mines] . . . as a 2.5 percent twelve-year loan. . . . The loan would long since have been paid off, and the $100 million which has gone into the Mudd philanthropies and the new empire for the Cyprus Mines Corporation could have been used to build a viable and rapidly expanding economy. And Harvey Mudd College under another name could have become one of the great educational institutions of the Mediterranean and Middle East.[26]

In many Third World countries, new leadership is emerging that challenges the existing pattern of foreign investment in their domestic economies. These new leaders realize that the long-run development of their countries will not be significantly aided by such exploitative arrangements and that until the developing country gains control over the direction of resource exploitation, true development will not occur. This new group advocates policies that would bring immediate or eventual national control of domestic resources, so that a viable economy can be developed.

Many countries are now seeking to negotiate a different sort of arrangement between themselves and their foreign investors. The ideal terms of such new arrangements might be that the investing company would agree to hire and train local people for its advanced management and engineering positions, to make higher tax payments, and to permit a gradual transfer of company control to a local public corporation within a specified period of years. What this would mean is that in return for a limited period of profit making, a foreign company would in effect agree to use its capital and expertise to launch an enterprise that would eventually be owned by the host country. Of course, the response of companies considering new investment is determined by the potential yield in profits of such an arrangement. If it seems to offer a good return on their money, they will invest; if not, they will go elsewhere. Since in the present world situation there are still many underdeveloped countries whose leaders are either greedy or apathetic enough to accept the foreign-investment situation as it is, the chances for arrangements more advantageous to the host country are still limited.

Most often, however, the issue of these new contracts is being contested between local governments and foreign investors who are already heavily involved in the economy. In such cases the host country has the advantage of legal sovereignty over the resources and can—sometimes with great difficulty—legally expropriate the assets and holdings of the outside companies. However, what is legal by local law may be regarded as piracy by the investors and their home countries, and the pressures that can be brought to bear on governments that consider such measures are enormous. I have already mentioned the economic blockade of Cuba. Another example is afforded by the former socialist government of Chile, which expropriated the major copper mines from their foreign owners (claiming that these countries had reaped immense profits from their sixty-year venture, profits exceeding the gross national product of Chile during that same period).[27] The expropriated foreign companies retaliated with legal and other pressures which made it virtually impossible for Chile to sell its copper in the international market.

The negotiations between Third World countries and their foreign investors over new terms of resource development can be difficult, highly political, and potentially disruptive of the local economy and the local government. Thus far the most successful of these negotiations have occurred between the oil-producing states and their foreign investors. The oil producers have been able to win terms which result in greater returns as well as in eventual control over the exploitation of their resources. As most commentators have observed, however, the situation of the Middle East oil producers is unique. They possess a highly desirable commodity; they are relatively safe from foreign military intervention, owing to the influence of the Soviet Union; and most of their member states are united in a common antagonism toward the state of Israel. These circumstances do not apply to the producers of commodities in other sectors, and thus the negotiating is much tougher.

Needless to say, behind these negotiations stand the respective countries of the investing companies. The United States, for instance, is quite willing to use its political, its economic, and at times its military power to support the claims of its corporations abroad. To return to the example of Chile, it has been revealed that the United States blocked grain sales, held up loans from the World Bank, financed opposition party leaders, and helped to underwrite a scheme to "destabilize" the country through strikes and protests.

A third tool that the United States and other developed countries can use for the assurance of "good relations" with Third World countries is *foreign aid*. Such assistance, in the form of grants, loans, and technical help, is often welcomed by developing countries since capital and expertise are usually needed to promote economic growth. The United States has long portrayed its foreign aid program to the American public and the world as a vast humanitarian project for the benefit of poor peoples. But the realities are quite different.

First of all, half our foreign aid, or about $5 billion a year, is in military assistance. Much of this is used to train and equip local militia and police forces to contain insurrection and discontent.[28] Second, virtually all of our aid is tied to an agreement that the Third World country will purchase our goods. Thus the United States Agency for International Development reported in 1971 that 99 percent of its grants was being spent on American goods. It added that 16.4 percent of all United States exports in iron and steel, 25 percent of all exports of fertilizer, and 15.7 percent of all exports of railroad equipment had been financed in that year with aid money and that termination of foreign aid would cost the country 70,000 jobs in the first year and 50,000 thereafter.[29]

Our much trumpeted Food for Peace program was based primarily on loans, not grants, enabling Third World countries to purchase excess agricultural commodities that had accumulated in United States warehouses as the result of our farm support program. These loans now amount to over $22 billion, all of which must be repaid by cash-starved developing countries. (In fact, the total debt burden of Third World countries from various United States, United Nations, and European aid programs is now a staggering $69.1 billion. When the additional debt contracted at market terms is added, the grand total for indebtedness in the Third World is $112 billion. The annual interest on these loans corresponds to 83 percent of all foreign aid.)[30]

Finally, United States aid has been used primarily to support American business and foreign policy interests. Addressing himself to a corporate audience in the *Columbia Journal of World Business,* former World Bank president Eugene Black enumerated the "dividends" of foreign aid: "(1) Foreign aid provides a substantial and immediate market for United States goods and services. (2) Foreign aid stimulates the development of new overseas markets for United States companies. (3) Foreign aid orients national economies toward a free enterprise system in which the United States firms can prosper."[31]

To this list his successor, George Woods, has added that foreign aid provides "tactical support of diplomacy" and assists in "holding military positions thought to be strategic."[32]

It has been part of United States political tradition that any good humanitarian should and would support the foreign aid program. Liberal senators could usually be counted on to cast their votes for it, and thousands of letters from globally oriented Americans would pour into Congress whenever foreign aid was threatened with reduction. In recent times, however, the self-serving, cynical use of the program has lost it more and more friends. One such disillusioned friend is United States Senator Frank Church, who announced in October of 1971 that he would no longer support it. "The major preoccupation of the present foreign aid program," he charged, "is the massive disbursement of munitions, and . . . to furnish American capital with a 'favorable climate for investment.' "

In his survey of the condition of the world's poor, people whom the United States aid program was supposedly helping, Senator Church found, as others have found, that the gap between the rich countries and the poor countries was growing—and that furthermore the gap between the rich elite in these countries and the vast majority of the people was also growing. He concluded that in many of these countries a "thoroughgoing social revolution" replacing the corrupt elite and bringing new, dedicated leaders was the only thing that could bring authentic development. But, he candidly observed,

in many underdeveloped countries, repressive governments draw reassurance from the arms we furnish and the military training we supply. [These] . . . regimes have neither the ability nor the interest to foster such a conception of social justice. They value aid from the United States as a means of maintaining, not of abolishing, inequalities of wealth and power. The lip service paid to reform is a crumb for their benefactors; it helps to make the Americans feel good and it costs them nothing.

In fact, American economic aid is commonly used to promote industrialization programs which generate a high level of consumption for the privileged, with little, if any, trickle-down benefit for the dispossessed. At the same time, American military assistance, and such military programs as the training and equipping of a country's police force, help such regimes. . . suppress reformist movements.[33]

Finally, in our survey of the tools the United States possesses for influencing the governments of Third World countries, we should not fail to mention *direct military intervention* and *covert operations* by the Central Intelligence Agency and other United States groups.

Whether the principle is referred to as the "Big Stick," the Monroe Doctrine, or the "Open-Door Policy," the United States has repeatedly made clear through word and deed that it is willing to intervene in other lands if significant American interests are threatened. Former Senator Everett Dirksen once pointed out that in the period between 1795 and 1945 the United States had directly intervened in other countries no less than 162 times—and he was including only interventions unauthorized by Congress.[34] Since 1945 the United States has intervened directly in Cuba, the Dominican Republic, Korea, Lebanon, Formosa, Vietnam, Laos, Cambodia, and Thailand. It has also supported covert military or paramilitary operations in Guatemala, Iran, Bolivia—and who knows how many other cases haven't come to light?

In addition to covert military operations, United States agencies have other, less conspicuous, methods of influencing governments—bribery, blackmail, and the like. The publication of the report of the Senate with regard to the involvement of the Central Intelligence Agency (CIA) in plots to assassinate the leaders of other nations constitutes an official acknowledgment by the United States Government of what has heretofore been a matter of rumor and accounts in world newspapers. As revelations concerning this "tool" of international diplomacy continue to emerge, it becomes increasingly impossible to believe that our support of repressive regimes abroad is accidental. On the contrary, it becomes self-evident that it is a major and deliberate component of American policy.

CONCLUSION

The facts which have emerged in our survey of the global economy speak for themselves, and the immorality involved in the relation between the First and the Third World need not be expatiated upon. Those of us who live comfortably in the rich world cannot avoid the knowledge that our affluence is based on the misery of the desperately poor.

Even if we turn from these people in callous disregard, we cannot escape the fact that our lifestyle, if left unchecked, will bring the world to ruin within our children's lifetime. So there seems no alternative, if we wish even to save ourselves, to the making of such substantial changes in the economic system as would amount to global redesign. But before endeavoring to indicate what directions this effort might take, I would like to move to a consideration of those who, within the present system, would seem to be the main beneficiaries of our global economy: the middle classes of the developed countries, and particularly the United States.

NOTES

1. William Moyer and Pamela Haines, "How We Cause World Hunger," *Win Magazine,* January 30, 1975.

2. Felix Greene, *The Enemy* (New York: Vintage, 1971), p. 151.

3. Ibid., p. 151.

4. See *The New Internationalist,* special population issue, October 1974.

5. *New York Times,* March 18, 1973.

6. Ibid.

7. Meadows et al., *The Limits to Growth,* p. 154.

8. *New York Times,* March 20, 1973.

9. Ibid., January 20, 1974.

10. Ibid., July 10, 1972.

11. Meadows et al., *The Limits to Growth,* p. 154.

12. *New York Times,* January 18, 1971.

13. Ibid., March 18, 1973.

14. Harry Magdoff, *The Age of Imperialism* (New York: Modern Reader, 1969), pp.49–50.

15. Falk, *This Endangered Planet,* p. 167.

16. Magdoff, *The Age of Imperialism,* p. 198.

17. *Jeremiad,* no. 35, October 25, 1971.

18. Frederick G. Donner, *The World-Wide Industrial Enterprise* (New York: McGraw, 1969), p. 15.

19. George Borgstrom, *The Hungry Planet* (New York: Collier Books, 1967), p. 284.

20. George Borgstrom, *Too Many* (New York: Collier-Macmillan, 1969), p. 237.

21. November 2, 1970, p. 58.

22. Ibid.

23. David Morris and Philip Wheaton, "Questions About Latin American Policy," *Christianity and Crisis,* June 22, 1970.

24. *Jeremiad,* no. 32, July 22, 1971.

25. Magdoff, *The Age of Imperialism,* p. 198.

26. Greene, *The Enemy,* pp. 169–71.

27. Advertisement taken by the Chilean government in the *New York Times,* January 25, 1971.

28. See the Senate Committee on Foreign Relations Five-Year Report, September 28, 1971, p. 8.

29. "Fact Sheets on Selected Aspects of United States Foreign Economic Assistance" (Washington, D.C.: Agency for International Development, 1972).

30. *Ceres,* January-February 1973, p. 21.

31. "The Domestic Dividends of Foreign Aid," *Columbia Journal of World Business,* vol. 1 (Fall 1965), p. 23.

32. Cited in "Farewell to Foreign Aid: A Liberal Takes His Leave," a Senate speech by Frank Church, October 29, 1971, in the *Congressional Record,* vol. 117, no. 162 (October 29, 1971), pp. S 17179 to S 17186.

33. Ibid.

34. *Congressional Record,* June 23, 1961.

4.   The Myth
of the Middle Class

At this point in our analysis of the global situation, the reader may well feel that we have finally isolated the villains on the world stage: the "middle classes" of the developed world and particularly the American middle class. For with respect to sheer numbers of people, aren't these the ones who are consuming so much, claiming such a disproportionate share of the world's resources? Aren't they the "enemy," and doesn't a global strategy for change simply involve knocking the props from under "their" system?

Well, yes and no. It is true that, figured on the basis of consumption, the middle classes represent the upper class of a world society. They, it seems, reap the rewards, while the rest of humankind hunger and toil. And yet, can it really be said that the present world economic order is "their" system? Do they really manage and control it, and is it designed to serve their needs and their happiness?

I think not. Privileged, yes. In control, no. In a very real sense it can be said that the middle classes, who seem at first sight to be the major beneficiaries of this system, are themselves caught in its grip; they have to run ever faster and faster to keep up with its demands and its cycles.

Writing in the *Christian Century*, John Raines expresses this truth in terms the reader will recognize:

The class that calls itself "middle" is in fact up against the wall; it is going nowhere—and neither are its kids.

Generally speaking, the takeoff point for "making it" in America comes only at the $25,000 a year line. That line is already beyond 95 percent of us (black and white together) and it is *constantly moving further away* under the double pressure of the majority crush below and the escalating concentration of wealth above. . . . Affluent? Comfortable? With the father holding two jobs and /or the mother working, our family will have to cope day after day with turmoil at home, defeat at the supermarket, and persistent exhaustion. No, there isn't much of a "middle" in America today. There is a top, and then there are all the rest of us pounding along on the endless stampede, wondering why we're always so tired.[1]

Is this just the lament of a privileged minority who, no matter how much is laid before them, will never be happy? Does this only serve to prove that humans are never satisfied? Are the complaints and distresses of the middle classes in America, Western Europe, and Japan something like the inhabitants of Versailles complaining about the heating or plumbing while the rest of humanity slaves in abject misery outside their royal walls?

No. Pitting the deprived masses of the underdeveloped and developed worlds against the middle classes seems like a neat solution, but in fact it ignores the real underlying principles of the system. I believe it would be far better to view the affluent middle classes as being similar to the house slaves in the ante-bellum South. Privileged, yes; and better-fed, better-clothed, and better-sheltered. But no more in actual control of the house or the larger plantation system than the common field slaves out in their shacks.

The central fact about the middle classes is this: that they are not, in fact, middle-class at all. They are middle-income workers, and while their physical lot is far, far better than that of their brothers and sisters in other parts of the world, they are still tied to the predominant economic machine with a short leash. When it coughs, they jump. When it no longer wants to produce what they are trained to manufacture, they adapt or sink. When it begins to ail, they feel the pain.

What I would contend is this: that the working classes of the developed countries, and the excluded millions in the Third World (except for China) are both—though not equally—at the mercy of the dominant economic institutional structure.

While at present they seem to be pitted against each other, they in fact have a common interest in seeing this system totally redesigned and democratized. It is presently controlled not by either of these groups, but by a handful of rich and powerful people whose unbridled pursuit of continued profits and dividends is going to bring us all to ruin.

In the rest of this chapter I will try to show how the middle-income worker is prodded and shaped by the dominant economic machine, and I will try to dispel the myth of the happy, stable "middle class" that has brought so much reassurance to an economic system challenged by humane and rational thinkers throughout the world.

A CONSIDERATION OF
NEW WORKING CLASS THEORY

The theory of the "new working class" is a concept or set of concepts that evolved during the 1960s in an attempt to understand the explosions that have occurred among students throughout the Western world. Perhaps the most significant and intriguing of all these revolts was the one that occurred in May of 1968 in France. There an alliance was formed between students, technical workers, and traditional workers —something that no one would have predicted, and which seemed to fly in the face of the hostility between workers and students that had been so clearly outlined in the United States.

The foremost thinker in this new school of class analysis is the Belgian Marxist Ernest Mandel. In 1968 he delivered a paper at the Socialist Scholars' Conference held at Rutgers University in New Jersey, and in this paper he tried to set out the reasons for the strange alliance that had occurred in France.[2]

Simply stated, his argument is this: white-collar workers—including engineers, health professionals, clerical workers, social workers, middle-level managers, government employees, and so on—represent a New Working Class in advanced industrial society. This New Working Class is similar to the old (i.e., blue-collar) working class in that its members essentially work for wages and are employed by large institutions which they do not own or control.

The "new" differs from the old working class in that it receives higher compensation (though the gap between the two is decreasing), is more highly educated, and thinks of itself as being "middle-class." Nevertheless, its essential interests are the same as those of the old working class, in that it is tied to wages and forced to seek employment in order to survive. As more and more of its members are forced into seeking work with large public or private institutions, they find that they have less and less to say regarding the outlines and nature of their tasks. More and more they discover that they are simply employees in a factory-like setting geared to the production of goods and services.

The theory goes on to state that this New Working Class is really just a new part of the old working class—that is, Marx's proletariat—though it may not yet be aware of it. Since the New Working Class is highly educated and is employed in the most technically advanced sectors of our society, it is the most capable of understanding the contradictions in our production-distribution system. It also realizes or could realize that as a class it is fully capable of running the machines and providing the services, eliminating any need for the rich and powerful managers and owners who determine how our resources will be used. This New Working Class is therefore the potential vanguard of revolution in advanced countries.

GETTING MARX STRAIGHT

Since many people today tend to reject Karl Marx out of hand, I would like to present a few considerations that may forestall quick criticism and rejection.

Marx believed, it will be recalled, that capitalism would develop to the point at which most of the society's wealth would be controlled by a very few, while the rest of the people would be reduced to laboring for these few. He predicted that the middle class would vanish and that the masses of the population would become part of the proletariat.

This proletariat, increasingly oppressed by having the fruits of its labor controlled and apportioned by others and by the necessity of submission to the edicts of its managers, and realizing that the workers themselves are the true producers of wealth, would finally revolt and take over the machinery of production: "The monopoly of capital becomes a fetter upon the mode of production. . . . Centralization of the means of production and socialization of labor at last reach a point where they become incompatible with their capitalist integument. The integument is burst asunder. The knell of private property sounds. The expropriators are expropriated."[3]

A number of thinkers have rejected Marx's prediction of the inevitable revolution on the basis of the evident fact that the middle class has not disappeared but has grown, while the blue-collar workers are not becoming increasingly oppressed and impoverished but, on the contrary, more powerful and more affluent.

William Ebenstein, professor of political science at Princeton, was certainly not the first to present this argument, but to a generation of college students raised on his political thinking in the 1950s and 1960s he is identified with it. In *Today's Isms,* a discussion of communism, fascism, capitalism, and socialism, Ebenstein argues that Marx has been proved fundamentally wrong by events. Far from growing, the number of proletarians has decreased, and a new group has emerged, the white-collar "salariat." The salariat, composed of salaried professionals and most types of service workers, is identified with the middle and upper classes. It is the leaven that will keep the revolution from occurring.[4]

We should recognize that Ebenstein uses the term "proletariat" in a way Marx did not. To Ebenstein the proletariat is equivalent to the ranks of blue-collar workers who are employed in factories to produce material goods. His definition is a very common one in American thought. Apparently it has been encouraged by the Communists themselves, since they have tended to laud the blue-collar worker as the only "real" worker, systematically ignoring the rising numbers of white-collar workers who differ only in being more educated (because modern capitalism requires more skilled and technical workers than in the past).

As for that other part of the folklore of communism, to the effect that the proletariat would become increasingly impoverished, there is this to say. It would seem to be contradicted by the increasing affluence of the American blue-collar worker. Nevertheless it is important to note the counter-argument Marxists have made. While it may be, they observe, that certain unionized sectors of the working class will carve out well-paying careers for themselves, these advances will be cancelled out by two responses on the part of the ownership class. The first is that the company in question will attempt wherever possible to shift the cost of wage increases onto the general public by raising prices, rather than sharing a greater percentage of their profits by absorbing these higher costs. The second is that the increasing tax burden of maintaining the welfare state—itself an attempt to cope with the cyclical stagnation of our economy—will be avoided by the influential and powerful and will come to rest on the backs of the working classes. Finally, it should be mentioned that with the inflation of the 1960s and 1970s, real wages have not appreciably risen, and in some sectors they have declined. In terms of purchasing power, some workers are worse off than they were five years ago; and with demands for four-day weeks, layoffs, and wage cuts, the working classes in the middle 1970s are fighting just to keep what they have already gained.

However, the proletarian status is not defined by the poverty of its condition but by its *relationship* to the means of production. When Marx talked about the oppression of the proletariat, he was referring to the oppression that comes from working in large institutions; from being one small part of a mechanized process, as functionally interchangeable as a cog or gear; from always having to work for someone else at a task someone else has set, rather than controlling your own life and your own work.

To Marx "middle class" had a very specific meaning: It

represented those people who owned the means of production—that is, factories or shops or farms that produced for sale. These were a true middle class because they owned property—that is, owned resources that would bring them a living without having to work for others. The people whom social commentators and the general public today call "middle class" are in fact simply middle-income workers, people who do not own any property in the Marxist sense but hire out like any common laborer and have their work determined for them by others.

Ebenstein himself recognized that his "salariat" was a rather odd group from the sociological point of view. While holding them up as a bulwark against communism, he could also say in a later section of his book that this very same group was the backbone of the fascist response in Germany and Italy. He was testifying to the inherent instability of this new group, an instability which consists in this: It has become identified with the old middle class and adopted middle-class and upper-class ideology; yet its objective social position is not middle-class in the former sense, but working-class—that is, proletarian.

THE NEED FOR A THEORY
OF THE NEW WORKING CLASS

Perhaps the classic work on this new group in the United States is C. Wright Mills's *White Collar,* first published in 1951, at the beginning of the spectacular post-war rise in salaried white-collar workers. Himself a Marxist, Mills found that he was not a little confused by the development of this new group; he wavered between an analysis of it as part of the working class or as something entirely different. This is reflected as a kind of ambiguity in his book. For when he terms them the "new middle class," the implication is that they could be recognized as part of the classical middle class; yet when he comes to describe their position and function in the working world, he sees them as people caught in the classical position of the proletariat:

When white-collar people get jobs, they sell not only their time and energy but their personalities as well. They sell by the week or month their smiles and their kindly gestures, and they must practice the prompt repression of resentment and aggression. For these intimate traits are of commercial relevance and required for the more efficient and profitable distribution of goods and services. Here are the new little Machiavellians, practicing their personable crafts for hire and for the profit of others, according to rules laid down by those above them.

In the eighteenth and nineteenth centuries, rationality was identified with freedom. The ideas of Freud about the individual, and of Marx about society, were strengthened by the assumption of the coincidence of freedom and rationality. Now rationality seems to have taken on a new form, to have its seat not in individual men, but in social institutions which by their bureaucratic planning and mathematical foresight usurp both freedom and rationality from the little individual man caught in them. The calculating hierarchies of department store and industrial corporation, of rationalized office and government bureau, lay out the gray areas of work and stereotype the permitted initiatives. And in all this bureaucratic usurpation of freedom and rationality, the white-collar people are the interchangeable parts of the big chains of authority that bind the society together.[5]

In 1951 Mills was truly a prophet in the wilderness. Too bad he couldn't have lived to see the eruption of the Free Speech Movement at Berkeley in 1964, when many of the underlying tensions he had seen only too clearly came bursting to the surface. For the revolt at Berkeley was an interesting mixture of a legitimate free-speech issue (political speakers and organizers were barred from the campus), a protest against educational regimentation, and a romantic and not very analytical rebellion against the work roles students were being prepared for.

The students at Berkeley, and even more the students who participated in the May 1968 revolt in France, recognized the post-war university for what it was: a highly organized and socially determined training center for functional jobs within the production system, in the government bureaucracies, in the health and welfare institutions, and in the educational institutions themselves. Colleges had become the preparation centers for a whole new stratum of the working class, and the students who were soon to go out and assume their rightful positions peopling the technocracy began to have second thoughts about the future that society had in store for them. For indeed weren't students reading letters of warning from those who had gone before them: *Death of a Salesman, The Organization Man, The Lonely Crowd?*

The student situation was this. On the one hand they had a clear awareness that they were being prepared to work for an economic system that many felt was the underlying cause of our present social and economic dilemma; on the other they were reading the poets, the philosophers—the creative writers who show that life is ever so much more than a home in the suburbs and a job with status. And four, sometimes seven, years to think about it. It was an explosive mixture. It still is.

A BRIEF LOOK AT THE UNITED STATES

So far, I have discussed New Working Class theory in more or less general terms, as it applies to the developed economies. It will be useful to consider the place of this group in the American economy, since there are few countries in which the proportion of salaried and educated workers is so high.

A recent Labor Department study has declared that by 1980 "there will be as many professional and technical workers as blue-collar workers" in the United States. In other words, the working population will be equally composed of "old" and "new" working-class elements. Former Labor Secretary Hodgson, who introduced the study to the press, concluded that this shift in employment opportunities would mean that education would be a more important factor in the job market than ever. He suggested that those workers with poor educations would find it harder than ever to enter the regular job market.[6]

What Mr. Hodgson did not discuss was the increasing evidence that the employment picture is not bright in the white-collar sector of the economy. The simple fact seems to be that we are producing more trained and educated workers than we are capable of using. The United States is rapidly developing a glut of high school- and college-educated workers and there is every indication that this situation is chronic. With the job market tightening in the schools, in the health and welfare institutions, in the technical and professional fields, we are finding that the bachelor's degree is no longer an automatic ticket into the job world, and that even graduate degrees are losing their market power. Youthful entrants to the job market are finding that meaningful and creative employment opportunities are rare, and that many are fortunate even to find jobs in the professions for which they trained.

The squeeze is on at the other end of the job market as well. Middle-aged workers are finding that they are expendable long before their productive life is completed. Managers, salesmen, engineers, researchers, and planners are all discovering that the availability of younger candidates who will work for less money has undercut their job security. And shifts in the economy have made many technical workers obsolete as companies have trimmed their rolls and reordered their investments.

Keith Bose, a technical writer for an aviation firm who was dismissed from his job at age forty-eight, is a good example of this new employment reality. His situation was described in a local Philadelphia newspaper. Jobless, Bose found that his assumptions of steady employment and rising affluence were shattered by the reality of an economy in which "the honest need for mechanical, electronic and other specialists was met long ago."

Bose used his forced retirement to study the plight of other workers like himself, and the conclusions of his study give chilling support to our analysis of the plight of the New Working Class:

Behind the facade of white stability lurks the haunting realization that the economy as presently constituted has a tragic surplus of white-collar workers. . . . Many of Richard Nixon's silent majority are discovering that only the thickness of a regular paycheck separates Middle America from the slum. In our preoccupation with the superfluous glitter of the affluent society, we have failed to discover that true affluence must be backed by ownership. *Middle America does not hold title to its affluence.* We are not true bourgeois, for we are unpropertied. We buy precarious status on time payments. Our chattels become worn-out and obsolete when title passes to us. Our "affluent" consumer economy is a vast parasite feeding on our earnings, and neither frugality nor industry will help us escape [emphasis added].[7]

Bose points to our increased productive capacity as a consequence of automated and cybernated techniques for manufacturing and for routine decision-making. As a major factor in cutting job opportunities he also cites the continued training of millions of new workers for nonexistent jobs and government policies that favor corporate investment but do not create jobs in proportion to the available labor pool.

The evidence seems to indicate that nothing short of a major reorganization of our economy will change this situation appreciably. The outlook for the future is one of increasing labor surplus in both blue- and white-collar sectors of the economy. This in turn means that college-educated and skilled workers are increasingly going to face the problems of frustration, job insecurity, and expendability that have been part of the blue-collar world for years.

Little wonder, then, that the fastest growth in unionization is occurring among the New Working Class. A recent survey taken by the *U.S. News and World Report* indicates that while blue-collar unions are stagnating, white-collar unions are growing by leaps and bounds. The membership of public employee unions has gone from 1 to 2.3 million since 1960 and the number of teachers working under union contract is up to 1.4 million. More than 50 percent of public employees are unionized, which certainly compares favorably with the national average of 27.5 percent for all workers.[8]

For anyone who reads the newspapers, it is hardly necessary to point out that not only have these white-collar unions grown in size, but they have grown more militant. This new militancy is a dramatic change from the quiescent attitudes of most white-collar employees just a few short years ago.

A classic example of this transformation are the public schoolteachers. In the 1950s, schoolteachers were the epitome of the respectable white-collar worker. Grossly underpaid, organized into school systems that functioned like factories, subject to the whims of the school board and school administrators, schoolteachers still clung desperately to the myth that they were somehow different from working class people. After all, they were college-educated, and they were seen as being of the upper or middle stratum by the communities in which they worked. They considered strikes and other union-like activities to be beneath their dignity as "professionals," and their professional associations reflected this attitude.

But in the 1960s the teachers began to develop some new ideas. Led by the big city teachers' unions—many of which had affiliated with the new American Federation of Teachers—school teachers began to go out on strike for higher wages and other union benefits.

The teachers have been followed by other public employees, notably the police, firefighters, sanitation workers, welfare workers, and hospital employees. If one adds the state, county, and municipal workers, the retail clerks, the postal employees union, and the clerical unions, we have a picture of a vital new force in the labor movement—one that is just beginning to sense its power and make its weight felt. This change in white-collar attitudes gives support to the Marxist belief that, in the long run, material conditions determine the ideological superstructure.

The New Working Class is discovering itself in the United States. Shaking off its "middle-class" identification, it is beginning to see itself as a part of the labor force, and its members are shedding their individualism for the very real benefits of collective action. With the gap between unionized white-collar and blue-collar workers decreasing, one can expect that a new "working class" consciousness will develop across the nation.

Marx foresaw the socialist revolution coming when the proletariat (the working class) recognized that it did not need the big capitalists any more, but could run things for itself, in other words, when social control of society's resources seemed to make more sense than private control. He expected this to occur in a mature capitalist society where the process of industrialization and proletarianization had occurred to such an extent that a very few controlled the resources while the great masses toiled for them.*

In this light, the Russian and Chinese revolutions were not the revolutions that Marx predicted. Marx looked to the United States and Great Britain for those revolutions. His analysis, I think, still holds up. We are playing out his drama right now, though it may take a good while before we reach the conclusion.

REFLECTIONS AND CRITICISMS

New Working Class theory is a powerful new tool for the analysis of our social system. It breaks the impasse that traditional "Marxist" analysis of industrial society placed us in by giving us a clear and relevant picture of the major development that has taken place in the work force since World War II. "End-of-ideology" liberals and non-Marxist radicals are undercut by its lucid explanations of the forces at work in modern society. The illusion of the Great American Middle Class is shattered by this more profound understanding of economic relationships in the United States.

The proletariat—that portion of society which Marx predicted would be the vanguard of the revolution and which in popular belief was supposed to have vanished—re-emerges in a new and important light. Fully nine-tenths of those who are today employed and their families can say: "The proletariat? That's me."

---

*It is important here to note that ownership is not the same as control, at least not in a corporate capitalist economy. Anyone who owns stock in a company may be said to "own" a portion of that company; yet what he or she actually owns is a certificate of title to a generally fixed share of the profits. Company policies are not set by the stockholders, but instead are determined by a handful of people elected by a small group of important stockholders. Often these important stockholders do not even hold a large percentage of the stock, much less a majority. Nevertheless, they manage through a number of devices—including the incredible difficulty of a proxy fight—to retain control of the company.

Therefore, those who argue that Marx was wrong because more and more people own shares in American industry are themselves missing the point. The rich don't have to "own" the corporations in order to control them and direct their policies to their primary benefit. (For an excellent discussion of this, see Adolf A. Berle and Gardiner C. Means, *The Modern Corporation and Private Property* [New York: Harcourt, 1968].)

Charles Reich, author of *The Greening of America,* was one of the first writers to sound this theme in its awesome and compelling simplicity:

> Today, in greatly varying degrees, we are all employees of the Corporate State and, what is more, exploited employees who sacrifice ourselves, our environment, and our community for the sake of irrational production. There is no class struggle; today there is only one class. In Marx's terms, we are all the proletariat, and there is no longer any ruling class except the machine itself.[9]

Reich's belief that "nobody" is running the machine —because the rich also are oppressed and unhappy and manipulated by the workings of our corporate system—is naive and overoptimistic, even though it contains a germ of truth. There seems little evidence that the "power elite" (the wealthy, the top managers, the military leaders) have any intention of relinquishing their control over the direction of the economy, even if their members all do have ulcers and weak hearts and secretly yearn for a good roll in the grass. His announcement of the burial of the class struggle is, I believe, a bit premature.

Yet granting that there may still be an upper class in industrial society, are we justified in saying that there is only one other class—the proletariat—and that we are all members of it?

I think not. I believe that Reich put his finger on a very important piece of reality when he proclaimed that we are all working for the machine and have nothing to lose but our false consciousness. This statement keys in to a crucial aspect of what life in the corporate, managed society is all about: that somehow we are all at the mercy of a system that makes *us* work for *it,* rather than the other way around.

It is premature, however, to assume that because we are all in some way oppressed by the operation of the system we therefore have a common indentification with each other or an equal stake in changing the system. There is a vast gulf between a $2.50-an-hour laundry worker and a $20,000-a-year manager (or a $12,000-a-year social worker).

Some of us profit more from this system than others—or, to put it the other way around—some of us are more oppressed by it than others. If concrete changes in our production and distribution system meant that some of us might have to give up certain present material benefits so that all of us could have a saner, healthier, happier society, we might well find that many "proletarians" would much rather have things stay the way they are.

There is no reason to assume that because our long-term interests are intimately bound together we will all join hands to change the system for the benefit of all. If history provides any clue, it seems far more likely that we will each continue to fight for our own immediate self-interest, joining with others only when we absolutely have to. The history of the labor movement is instructive on this point. The political thrust of the labor movement has often been in the direction of helping all workers and their families. Social Security, minimum wage legislation, factory safety laws, and civil rights legislation are all examples of programs that have benefited workers in general. On the other hand, unions have used the closed shop and the apprenticeship system to exclude minorities from their ranks. They have also created privileged positions for their members, with high wages and good benefits, while restricting their membership. Labor unions have been particularly unsympathetic to farm and migrant workers, many of whom are still not covered by minimum wage legislation, and there are at present no strong indications that the new white-collar unions are more mindful than their blue-collar predecessors of others' needs; indeed, they may be less so.

If we jettison the idea of a strong and growing "middle class" in America, it does not automatically follow that we can proceed to lump everyone but the rich in the proletariat. As we have pointed out, we are all manipulated by the corporate economy, but some benefit more than others. And even if we can say that the system is run by and for the very rich, some of us benefit more from its present organization than do others. This is the thesis proposed by Norman Birnbaum and Stanley Aronowitz, two political analysts who have each tried to look at the operations of modern industrial society with an eye to the possibilities for social change.

Writing independently, the two authors have come up with a five-class or five-stratum model for industrial society. They identify (1) a lumpenproletariat class, composed of the transitory migrant worker and those on welfare; (2) a traditional working class, which may or may not be viewed as including both blue- and white-collar workers; (3) a managerial class, composed of the highest-paid professionals; (4) an old middle class, composed of traditional middle-class elements such as small-scale manufacturers, independent professionals, and shopkeepers; and finally (5) an upper class or elite which holds the reins of power and has vast wealth at its disposal. Both authors suggest that any strategy for social change will have to take the interest of these varying groups into account.[10]

It is possible to take the stratification of Birnbaum and Aronowitz onto a world scale. There we would find the majority of humankind in what they call the lumpenproletariat stratum—people whose lives are essentially lived outside the wage system of industrial production but are nevertheless profoundly affected by the workings of that system. Within this group fall the hundreds of millions who lead subsistence lives on the land or in the world's cities.

A second stratum is composed of the industrial and agricultural workers of the world—people who work for wages and produce commodities for the use of others. Such a grouping includes Bolivian tin miners with Canadian steel workers, underpaid South Korean textile workers with highly paid European engineers. It also includes the educational and service workers who receive wages to keep the system going —schoolteachers, social workers, public employees.

A third stratum is composed of traditional middle-class elements—professional people, the owners of small and medium-sized farms and of small businesses, shops, etc.

A fourth stratum is composed of people who make up local and national power-elite groupings—the owners of large farms and medium-sized businesses, military leaders in countries without internationally significant power, and politicians.

A fifth stratum consists of the international power elite —i.e., those people who are so rich and powerful that their decisions affect the course of global development. This stratum includes the political leaders of the major countries, the top managers of the giant multinational corporations, the very rich, and military leaders of countries having significant international power.

The vast bulk of humankind is found in the first two categories: those employed in the market economy and those who gain a subsistence living on its edges. If we had a world democracy, these people would hold the majority of votes. When we talk about betterment for the mass of humankind, it is through them that this betterment will be measured. These people run the machines, plant the crops, staff the armies, dig in the mines.

But it is obvious that decision making with regard to world development does not rest in the hands of these first two strata; it is instead almost exclusively in the hands of the international power elite. This elite is not unified in much other than a desire to maintain its powerful positions and, if possible, extend them. Thus the American power elite and the Japanese power elite may see eye-to-eye on some international matters but be in disagreement over others. And Soviet and American leaders may want to continue their role of limited collaboration as great powers in international political affairs, yet come into conflict over the Middle East.

Similarly, it can hardly be said that the working classes of the world are united in purpose. One might well feel that it is more realistic to separate a grouping of highly paid workers in the affluent countries from lower-paid workers in their home countries and abroad. After all, an American automobile worker would seem to benefit more from the system than a Brazilian coffee worker—and in some ways the former may be said to benefit at the expense of the latter. And it may well be said that the industrial workers of developed and developing nations as well find their interests opposed to those of the lumpenproletariat, who are pressing for a greater share of the world's goods, and to those of the farm workers, who are supplying the food.

In the midst of all this stand the average Americans: working for a living; tied to jobs that may be useless, unnecessary, or environmentally damaging; trying to make ends meet when food prices keep rising and the family auto lasts only to the end of the final installment; watching the environment deteriorate all around them; aware of the world hunger problem and increasingly of the world resource problem and wondering what, if anything, can be done.

And so we come full circle. We are an "upper class"; we are a "middle class"; we are "the proletariat." We exploit and are exploited. We consume and are ourselves consumed. To understand ourselves and the existential, moral, and personal dilemma we face, we must see ourselves as sinners and sinned against, as participants in and as beneficiaries of the dominant economic system, and yet as victims of it as well.

And the question we face is this: Are we willing to change our lifestyles? Even more: Are we willing to throw in our lot with the bulk of humankind and work together with them to bring about a better world order? Or will we decide to try to hold onto the benefits of the present system—as immoral and as irrational as it may seem, and as dangerous as that decision is in the long run?

This is not a question that I or anyone else can answer now. All that can be done is to point out that even the affluent groups in the world system may stand to benefit by a substantial change in its workings. In my chapter on global redesign I shall attempt to sketch some ideas about how such a new system might look and what changes might be of benefit to the currently privileged. Whether there is a commanding vision capable of somehow uniting enough of the world's people to make the necessary changes, and whether the American working classes will be part of this movement—or a major hindrance to it—are questions that can be answered only by time and by the efforts of people of good will throughout the world.

And yet there are signs of the time: so I would interpret the findings of a recent Harris Survey, reported in the *New York Post* of December 1, 1975. I quote the data most relevant to our present inquiry:

A solid, 61–23 percent majority of the American people feels it is "morally wrong" that Americans, who comprise only 6 percent of the world's population, consume 40 percent of the world's energy and raw materials. . . .

Gnawing at the affluent conscience of this country is the judgment by 68 percent of the public that we are "highly wasteful." Indeed, only a bare 5 percent think we are "hardly wasteful at all." By 90–5 percent, a nearly unanimous public believes that "we here in this country will have to find ways to cut back on the amount of things we consume and waste."

By 81–10 percent, the public also feels that excessive consumption "causes us to pollute the air, the rivers and the seas."

Only 42 percent now think it is essential for the country to "create a desire on the part of consumers to buy new products." By contrast, a much larger 61 percent feel it is very important "to bring more modern and better services to an increasing number of people."

More than six out of every ten people employed in the country now work in service industries, and not in the manufacture of products. The thrust of the latest Harris Survey findings is that this trend toward a service economy will accelerate.

A major question, of course, is how much the standard of living will drop if Americans cut back on consumption. By 64–29 percent, a majority anticipates a reduction in living standards if wasteful consumption is to be brought under control.

The implications of these results . . . could well be sweeping and significant. They suggest that Americans may face a rapidly changing lifestyle where the accumulation of physical possessions and steadily increasing consumption would no longer be as central to people's concerns as in the past. This would mark a striking turnabout in the country's thinking.[11]

Can there be a way of living as an adult in this society that even begins to respond to the problems all around us? Is there, to be precise, a lifestyle of integrity for our time? It is to this question that I would now like to turn.

NOTES

1. "Middle America: Up Against the Wall and Going Nowhere," May 2, 1973.

2. "Workers Under Neo-Capitalism," *International Socialist Review*, November-December 1968, pp. 1–16.

3. Quoted in Louis B. Boudin, *The Theoretical System of Karl Marx*, 1st ed. 1907; reprinted by Monthly Review Press (New York, 1967), p. 218.

4. *Today's Isms*, 3rd ed. (Englewood Cliffs, N.J.: Prentice-Hall, 1961).

5. New York: Galaxy, 1956, p. xvii.

6. *New York Times*, November 11, 1970.

7. *Philadelphia Inquirer*, June 13, 1971.

8. "Is the Labor Movement Losing Ground?" February 21, 1972.

9. New York: Random, 1970, p. 310.

10. "Strategies for Radical Social Change: A Symposium," *Social Policy*, November-December 1970, comments by Stanley Aronowitz, pp. 10–13; see also Norman Birnbaum, *The Crisis of Industrial Society* (New York: Oxford University Press, 1969).

11. "Poll: U. S. Consumption Morally Wrong," under the byline of Louis Harris.

II. THE SIMPLE LIVING MOVEMENT

"I commit myself to join with others in the reshaping of institutions in order to bring about a more just global society in which all people have full access to the needed resources for their physical, emotional, intellectual, and spiritual growth."

—THE SHAKERTOWN PLEDGE

5. The Shakertown Pledge

On April 30, 1973, a group of religious retreat center directors and their staffs gathered at the site of a restored Shaker village about forty miles south of Lexington, Kentucky. We were there, at Shakertown at Pleasant Hill, for the annual Retreat Center Directors' Fellowship, a gathering which usually draws twenty or thirty people from various points in the East and Midwest for a few days of swapping stories, comparing programs, and renewing old friendships. It is designed to be a forum, nothing more, and whatever joint efforts or new program directions come out of it are considered to be unexpected, if welcome, dividends.

But this year something different happened. After a day of lively discussion on such current issues as the Charismatic movement and the growth of religiously-oriented encounter groups, we decided to take a few minutes to talk about "a global perspective on our efforts." The talk turned to the alarming statistics about world need and world resources and our possible response as Americans and Christians. When we were only a few minutes into the discussion, I suddenly realized that the atmosphere had changed from the light-heartedness with which we had begun. Some people seemed bored, some angry; some had become intensely serious, and still others seemed quietly agonized.

I had seen similar reactions before, particularly on those occasions when the focus of the discussion had been on how each of us was conducting our own life in the light of the very real needs of the world.

Those of us who were sitting in that room knew that we were part of the privileged minority of the world's population and that the people we worked with and ministered to also belonged to that small "upper class." We may not all have been aware of the statistic that an estimated fifteen thousand people die every day in the world from malnutrition, but we were keenly aware that other people went hungry while we ate well. Not all of us, perhaps, had realized that our consumption of resources is such that the world could not possibly afford another United States; but we did know that our nation was guilty of overconsuming the world's resources and that our own lifestyles were part of the problem. For the world, notwithstanding its exotic corners, is no longer a mystery too vast for ordinary people to fathom. Through television and radio it has become a global village, and we, the favored inhabitants, were only too well aware of our special status.

Yet this subjectively felt guilt is not matched by an objective solution to the world's problems. Granted that our lifestyles involve overconsumption, would any lessening of our pace materially benefit others? If I eat less, how do I know that someone else will necessarily be able to eat more? If we spend less, won't that harm our economy, and perhaps bring its collapse? How could that aid anybody?

The global village is not a simple place. The contrasts seem stark enough, as does the need for reorganization and redistribution. But the solutions are hardly plain, and the complexities engender tremendous frustration.

Therefore people tend to freeze when this subject is raised. They do what laboratory test animals do when presented with an apparently insoluble problem: They get depressed, they pretend the problem doesn't exist, or they run around in circles.

But this time it was different. Sam Emerick, chairperson of the conference and until recently the director of the Yokefellow Institute, said: "Listen, this is a gut issue for me. It's something that I've been thinking about and agonizing over for some time now. I don't want to just talk about it. I want to *do* something." There were a number of us who felt similarly, and after the meeting closed we gathered somewhat excitedly to see what we could come up with.

We decided to meet again at the Yokefellow Institute in Richmond, Indiana. By the time we arrived, we already felt that we were committed, not just to some lofty proclamation about the world's problems, but to try to do something about it in the "institutional arena" and in our own lives. After two days of talking and praying, and a subsequent period of correspondence and of drafts and redrafts, we agreed on a common pledge which we would take together and commend to others. We called it the Shakertown Pledge in honor of our original gathering place and because the Shaker community had believed wholeheartedly in lives of "creative simplicity." Here is what we agreed upon:

Recognizing that the earth and the fulness thereof is a gift from our gracious God, and that we are called to cherish, nurture, and provide loving stewardship for the earth's resources,
and recognizing that life itself is a gift, and a call to responsibility, joy, and celebration,
I make the following declarations:
   1. I declare myself to be a world citizen.
   2. I commit myself to lead an ecologically sound life.
   3. I commit myself to lead a life of creative simplicity and to share my personal wealth with the world's poor.
   4. I commit myself to join with others in the reshaping of institutions in order to bring about a more just global society in which all people have full access to the needed resources for their physical, emotional, intellectual, and spiritual growth.
   5. I commit myself to occupational accountability, and so doing I will seek to avoid the creation of products which cause harm to others.
   6. I affirm the gift of my body and commit myself to its proper nourishment and physical well-being.
   7. I commit myself to examine continually my relations with others, and to attempt to relate honestly, morally, and lovingly to those around me.
   8. I commit myself to personal renewal through prayer, meditation, and study.
   9. I commit myself to responsible participation in a community of faith.

The first thing that can be seen about this pledge is that there is no mention of Jesus Christ. This was deliberate. We decided that we wanted to formulate a "basic" pledge that would be acceptable to all those who wanted to live religiously responsible lives.* For our part, we wanted to proclaim to the religious community our conviction that God is calling us to a new "lifestyle" for our times.

We decided that the Pledge could, and should, be rewritten by various religious communities that felt moved by its call, so that it would reflect their own most meaningful confessional language. The important thing about the Pledge is the idea, not any particular brand or version.

WHAT DOES IT MEAN?

People who have seen the Shakertown Pledge have reacted most strongly to its two "sacrificial" points (numbers 2 and 3). It was our hope that they would. Declarations of world citizenship are not new. Devotional commitments are important, but are hardly new. What is "new" in the Pledge—and what gives it impact—is the firm declaration that personal piety, social conscience, and a simple lifestyle are all essential parts of a religious life that possesses integrity.

What we have in mind is not "holy poverty"—or, as one friend put it, "a St. Francis trip"—though we deeply respect those people who feel led to make such radical commitments. We thought carefully about the phrase "creative simplicity"; in fact, it was chosen in preference to the word "frugality," which has a pinched, miserly ring to it in modern parlance.

What the Pledge envisions is not a wholesale renunciation

---

*In addition to the Reverend Samuel Emerick, the original formulators of the Pledge include the Reverend Brant Loper and the Reverend James Simmons, then both at Yokefellow Institute; the Reverend Stephen Sebert and Mrs. Mary Perdue of Yokefellows at Shakertown; David Hartsough of the Simple Living program of the Northern California office of the AFSC; Phyllis and Richard Taylor of the Life Center in Philadelphia; Mrs. Janet Shepherd and myself, then from Kirkridge Retreat Center in Pennsylvania; Dr. William Clemmons and Dr. Harvey Hester of the Vineyard Conference Center in Louisville, Kentucky; the Reverend Keith Hosey and Sister Maureen Mangen of the John XXIII Center in Indiana; and Dr. Richard Baer, now a faculty member at Cornell University. Our personal endorsement of the Pledge did not necessarily represent an institutional commitment to it.

of all material goods and a life of ragged poverty. We don't want people to feel guilty every time they go to a movie or eat a handful of popcorn. What we do want, though, is that all of us should look at our lifestyle in the light of our faith and the very real needs of the rest of the world. The Pledge asks that we each take time to consider what things are really necessary in our lives for happiness and joy and health and survival. It asks that we use our expanded consciousness and loving concern to constantly discern new ways to live out this commitment. Finally, it asks that we try to free as much of our money as possible, so that this wealth can be transferred to people and lands that desperately need it.

We believe that an ecologically sound, creatively simple lifestyle is important for three reasons: first, so that our own lives can be more simple and gracious, freed from excessive attachment to material goods; second, so that we are able to release more of our wealth to share with those who need the basic necessities of life; third, so that we can begin to move toward a Just World Standard of Living, in which we are not consuming more of the earth's resources than is our due.

To those of us who have taken the Pledge, each point has importance and significance. The other points of the Pledge (in addition to 2 and 3) were not thrown in for religious window-dressing. The nine points combine to form a picture of what we think it means to *live* one's faith in these times.

We believe that deep and continuing personal renewal can result from a discipline of prayer or meditation. We believe that God not only has a relationship with each of us individually, but with us also collectively—as a "people"—and we hold that common worship and the support of a community of common beliefs are essential to an active, creative, and joyous life. We affirm many of the contributions of the small-group movement in the church, especially in the area of increased sensitivity to others and increased appreciation of oneself.

Finally, we believe that it is imperative for all concerned people to work actively in the institutional and political arena to try to bring about major changes in the relationship between the rich nations and the poor nations. There is a necessity for wealthy nations, such as the United States, to redesign those parts of their economies that are wasteful and harmful in ecological terms. We must work strenuously to end poverty within the borders of our own country; and at the same time we must reduce our overconsumption of scarce resources, while lending our support to the ecologically sound development of the poor nations, to the end that the basic needs of all the passengers of "spaceship earth" shall be equally fulfilled.

This means that we will vote—and perhaps campaign both here and abroad—for the political candidate who will do most for the poor. It may mean that we will engage in lobbying, in peaceful demonstrations, and in other forms of "direct action" in support of efforts to construct a more just global economic order. It means that we will oppose and attempt to change those aspects of our economic system that create an unjust distribution of wealth and power here and abroad.

THE RESPONSE

The reaction to the Shakertown Pledge was swift and encouraging. "I believe that this is the best formulation of a Christian lifestyle that I have seen," wrote a Methodist pastor from California. "We are excited to find something like the Pledge," wrote a couple from Michigan. "It affirms everything that we are doing and gives us hope that others are moving in the same direction." Letters began to pour in from all over the country and all over the world, letters of praise, letters of encouragement, letters of people who felt for the first time that they were not alone.

The first public notice of the Pledge appeared in an article in the April 1974 issue of *Fellowship,* a religious and pacifist magazine. Religious News Service then picked up the story, and soon word of the Pledge was appearing in denominational magazines and Sunday bulletins across the country. Requests for copies, for more information, for speakers, for advice all began to flow into our office, and we realized that we had touched a very important nerve in the American religious body.

People began to make their own copies of the Pledge, some with our address, some with local postings. Several groups tried their hands at rewording it. One man painted the entire Pledge on his wall—the better to contemplate its meaning!

Individual response was followed by institutional response. In June of 1974 a gathering of prominent religious leaders commended the Pledge in their final report, after a three-day consultation on "global justice." In California the social action committee for the Methodists' northern region decided to develop Simple Living study groups in every Methodist church in their region. The Episcopalians sent the Pledge out to their national network of adult study leaders. Several Catholic religious congregations considered the Pledge as a focus for congregational effort. And a gathering of sixteen major Protestant denominations, brought together to consider the world food problem, called their congregants to consider lives of "creative simplicity."

Quickly the Pledge became a "consciousness raiser" and an organizing tool. Churches found that it provided a perfect study document for adult and youth groups. Workshops and conferences on world hunger often ended with a presentation of the Shakertown Pledge and a call for members to consider signing it. "Renewal" retreats were organized around the question of "lifestyle," and the Pledge was used to help shape people's thinking.

Finally, we found that there was a tremendous interest on the part of clergy and laity in learning methods for presenting new lifestyle options to congregations. By November of 1974 we had organized our first Simple Living Organizers' Training Workshop and had shared our skills and information with thirty people from all over the East and Midwest. Several more workshops followed, and plans were laid for a national series around the country (and in Canada).

By the end of the first year of effort, several hundred people had signed the Pledge, thousands had studied and been challenged by it, and millions had seen it (one United Nations publication even carried it in five languages). For many it was a formulation of a creed they had already adopted; for others it was a final impetus for lifestyle change; for still others it was perhaps the first time they had been challenged to consider seriously a major change in their lifestyle.

Not all reactions were immediately positive. "This thing threatens the hell out of me," said one candid campus minister at a gathering in Ann Arbor. "And the damnedest thing about it is that it leaves it up to the individual conscience."He was part of a gathering of campus ministers from around the country that I addressed on the Pledge. Sophisticated, urbane, prone to support good causes, these campus ministers were a group I had looked to for enthusiastic support. But I was sadly disappointed. When I introduced the Pledge and asked them to consider applying it to their own lives, the room fell strangely silent. Caught themselves in the middle-class lifestyle, these men and women found themselves baffled and not-so-slightly uncomfortable. I had earlier told them that I felt no seriously religious person would be able to avoid the challenge of the Pledge within three years time. Most seemed glad that they had three years until the day of reckoning!

Other people felt that the Pledge was too "easy." They would criticize its general language and question whether anyone would really be challenged by signing it. To that question we found that the answer was an unqualified yes. People were very much challenged by the Pledge and sensed intuitively what it was calling for. Its open-ended quality didn't let people off the hook; instead it constantly prodded them to consider further simplicity. "Some days I'm sorry I ever signed that thing," one of the original formulators told me. "I think about it every time I go to spend money."

Finally, there were people who felt that the Pledge wasn't "political" enough. Those who signed it, they argued, would be allowed to feel good about changing their lifestyle, when political action for international social change was what was really called for. They feared that people who signed the Pledge would consider that they had "done their part" and ignore the needed social-action involvements.

There is no easy answer to this last question. We *do* know that many of the people who have signed the Pledge are already involved in social-change work at the local, national, and international level. We *do* know that the people who respond to the challenge of the Pledge are generally only too aware of the need for global redesign of institutions and processes. But whether the Shakertown Pledge is able to focus and galvanize a broad religious movement for global justice is a question only time can answer.

THE NEXT STEP

There is already a Simple Living movement in the country. It is composed of youthful "dropouts" who have gone to live on farms in the country and middle-aged professionals who have decided to quit the "rat race." It finds adherents among Catholic nuns and secular anarchists. It gathers together the middle-American Christian family and Zen Buddhist monastics. At present it is largely a white movement with primarily middle-class members; but, for the moment, perhaps this is as it should be. It is, after all, the middle and upper classes in America today who have the most to give away.

Those who practice simple living would agree that it frees energy for important things: It is healthier, less emotionally taxing, and more personally satisfying than the typical middle-class existence for many people. It is less wasteful, and more in harmony with nature. Those who live simply are aware that they are creating more room for others, and potentially freeing needed resources.

Whether the Simple Living movement is going to be a major force for social change or just another middle-class lifestyle "option" depends in large part on whether the participants themselves are willing to wrestle with the economic and social implications of their "radical" witness and whether they are willing to engage in political activity to help bring a new society into being.

The practitioners of simple living are going to have to ask themselves what their advice would be to the eight million people of New York City, or the six hundred million people of India. They are going to have to consider how the world's scarce resources can be equitably divided among the world's people. By examining their own sources of support—how they got their land, or their houses, or their tractors—they may be led to ponder how the two billion poor inhabitants of the world will get *their* initial capital for living simply. Finally, it is only fair to ask those who have chosen to live simply to look at the global multinational/military power complex, seeing how it systematically robs Third World countries and keeps their populations in subjection—with much of the resultant benefit flowing to us.

The Shakertown Pledge represents an attempt to bring together two factors for social change: a concrete vision of a new society and a radical willingness to begin living for that society now. It takes the intuitive insights of the Simple Living movement and tries to develop them into a complete vision of a new future. It asks the more quiescent members of the Simple Living movement to become politically conscious and active; and it asks the politically aware to reshape their life-styles into consonance with their beliefs.

It is only a beginning. And it is designed to allow many people from many different walks of life and different political persuasions to share its basic tenets. The real question for the Shakertown Pledge, and the idea behind it, is whether those who are caught up in its vision will be willing and able to give impetus to a broad and powerful movement for global justice—one that will speak to the imagination of the world's people and capture it.

In the remainder of this book I will try to develop a particular line of commentary on the Shakertown Pledge, one that summons Christians to a new lifestyle and our church to a new institutional style. For the sake of the diversity and range of people who have been and are responding to the Pledge, I want to stress that the arguments given and positions taken in the following chapters are the fruit of my own reflection on the Shakertown Pledge (plus a lot of help from my friends!) and do not represent the official, or even the unofficial, stance of the Shakertown Pledge Group. *

———

*See Appendix A and Appendix B for more commentary on the Shakertown Pledge.

6. Toward a Just World Standard of Living

SIMPLICITY

One of the first questions those of us involved with the Simple Living movement are asked is "How simple is simple?" People naturally want to know what new standard they are being called to, and whether it seems within the realm of possibility. To answer this question we find that we have to discuss simplicity in two distinct, though related, dimensions. The first might be called the "private" dimension. This aspect of simplicity has to do with our ability to let go—to detach ourselves from material possessions, and even from the desire for them. Traditionally , the religious emphasis on simplicity has tended to be focused on this dimension: simplicity, as it were, for the sake of one's own soul.

The second dimension might be called the "social," the sphere of one's relationships with others. This call to simplicity is not so much for the sake of one's own soul as for the sake of others, especially for their real physical needs. The ecological crisis adds a new urgency to this argument for a simplified lifestyle, as does the growing awareness of the world food problem.

The two dimensions are, of course, related. Jesus tells the

story of the rich man, Dives, and Lazarus, the poor beggar outside his door whom he had ignored, to show that one's soul is truly in peril if one denies the needs of others. Since the poor have been present in virtually all societies for most of human history, the call to Christians to live simply so that they could share with others was there from the beginning. Since the "Christian" nations are among the world's wealthy elite, this call is even stronger in our time.

In this chapter I would like to review briefly the arguments for simplicity in both the "private" and the "social" dimensions. Beyond that, I would like to suggest that there may very well be an objective, measurable, standard of living to which all persons of wealth are called. Going even one step further, I will argue that there is a just standard of consumption for *nations,* and that we Christians are called to move our nation toward this new ethical standard.

The Private Dimension

"If you wish to go the whole way," Jesus told the rich young man, "go, sell your possessions, and give to the poor" (Matt. 19:21).* Going "the whole way" meant, of course, the "letting go" we are talking about. It meant becoming free to follow Jesus and gaining eternal life. That is, after all, what the rich young man desired , and he was assured by Jesus that if he did let go of his possessions he would have "riches in heaven." This is the meaning of "private" simplicity in our time. The young man was inquiring about his own spiritual state, and Jesus' response was that his riches were a barrier between him and God. Obviously Jesus' insight was precise because we are told that when the young man heard this, "he went away with a heavy heart; for he was man of great wealth" (v. 22).

"Perfection," "holiness," "justification," "righteousness"— these traditional terms in the discussion of the spiritual life are so historically "loaded," that I would like to suggest others.

---

* *The New English Bible: New Testament.* All excerpts from the New Testament are quoted from this edition.

How about "wholeness," or "spiritual aliveness," or "fullness in the Spirit"? Then, spelled out, what Jesus is saying to the young man is this: If you want to be a complete human being, if you want to *know* the presence of God in your life, then sell all your possessions. . . . Perhaps for some of us this kind of formulation will come closer to our own inner language of spiritual yearning.

In any event, it seems clear that in this story Jesus was not emphasizing the young man's social relationships. He was not denouncing him as an oppressor of the poor, or criticizing his stewardship of the riches he possessed. What he was telling the young man was that his wealth was getting in the way of his own full spiritual development.

"Wherever your treasure is," Jesus tells us, "there will your heart be also." The rich young man obviously had a divided heart. He wanted to live a holy life, but he also wanted to hold onto his wealth. He wanted, in effect, to serve two masters.

Looking at our own lives with reference to simplicity, then, we must begin with the question, What is our treasure?—that is, what do we have our hearts set on? There is such a variety of things we can set our hearts on: getting rich, staying rich, or getting richer; succeeding in a certain career, or becoming famous, or having a nice farm in the country; having a family, or proving something to our parents—or changing the world. Whatever our treasure is, if it comes before God in our hearts, then it must be "given away."

I have an exercise I often use with retreat groups. As a preparation for meditation, I ask them to consider the following situation: Suppose God came to you in your sleep one night and asked you to undertake a great mission. Suppose God said that you were to begin that very night, getting up from your bed and walking out—perhaps never to return. What would you be afraid to leave? Would it be your house? your family? your plans for the future?

Whatever comes first to mind is your treasure. It is this that is capable of becoming a barrier between you and God.

Now be careful with this exercise. Just because our families come at once to mind does not mean that we have to leave them! Sometimes a vocation from God has involved that, but only rarely. We must love our families; but we must love God more. We must love our families not as "possessions," but as persons in themselves, belonging to God. So also with our worldly goods, our careers, our plans for the future, our ambitions. What is important is to begin to understand just where our heart is focused, and then try to free ourselves from that "possession," so that we can refocus on God. Freeing ourselves may simply mean that we come to understand why we have attached excessive importance to a certain possession, so that we are then able to "let go" of it—object, idea, or whatever else—emotionally. Only when we have become able to let go can we free ourselves of that possession as an obstacle between ourselves and God.

Returning to our earlier question—how simple is simple?—we can now say this: The ideal of Christian simplicity is to be free to follow God's leading. The more we are able to let go of our possessions, the closer we will be to wholeness—to being who God really wants us to be.

Obviously, what may be a serious obstacle for one person may be no barrier at all for another. That is why I don't assume that a person who happens to have an abundance of material possessions is further from God than a person who has few. I have met people surrounded by material wealth who have been willing to leave it all when God called them to a task. I have met others who, living in relative poverty, are so much attached to their few possessions—and to their desire for more—that they would be almost paralyzed if God were to call them to leave what they have. There is no *objective* measure of simplicity on the level of personal spiritual development, though it seems likely that the more possessions one has, the more likely it is that a strong attachment to them will form. We all must wrestle with our own particular attachments, we all must find our own way to being at peace with the world outside us.

In the social dimension, however, this is not true. Here it is clear that an objective standard of simplicity does exist and that it can be measured in dollars and cents. It is to this dimension that I would now like to turn.

The Social Dimension

"If a man has enough to live on, and yet when he sees his brother in need shuts up his heart against him, how can it be said that the divine love dwells in him?" (1 John 3:17). Charity has always been the hallmark of Christian ethics; not the charity that consists in giving from one's surplus, but that exemplified by the widow who gave part of the insufficient amount she had to live on (Mark 12:42–44). The basis for simplicity on the social plane—the dimension of our relationships with others—is given in the commandment to love our neighbor as ourselves. If we are to follow that commandment in these times, if we are really to love our neighbor as ourselves, we will recognize that the world is urgently in need of a simple lifestyle on the part of the people of God.

We are one world, and the resources of the earth are limited. What I consume relates directly to what is available for others; if I consume more than my fair share, I am literally taking food from the mouths of others, clothes from their bodies. Therefore if I am to follow God's commandments, to take Christ's teaching seriously, I must restrain my consumption of the world's resources.

Our relationships with other living things in the world is also to be taken into account—the fish, the fowl, the beasts of the earth. When God gave us "dominion" over the other living things of the world, this did not make us free to destroy creation—which is what we are doing now. Living a God-centered life in the social dimension also means, then, that we must stop destroying our wildlife and polluting the earth's waters and its atmosphere.

A JUST WORLD STANDARD OF LIVING

All that we have said thus far gives no more than certain indications of the directions a Simple Living movement should take. The question remains: Just how simple is simple? In an effort to come up with some kind of answer, those of us who are involved in the movement have developed a concept based on common sense. It is simple enough, on the face of it;

yet if it caught on, it might well have a revolutionary impact on global society. We call it the Just World Standard of Living, and what is involved is an effort to determine a level of consumption at which people would not be taking more than their fair share of the world's resources.

It stands to reason that if the world's resources can, roughly, be quantitatively measured, then there must be such a thing as a just standard of living—a level, universally applied, at which they will be equitably distributed to all the world's people. As will shortly be seen, this standard is not easy to arrive at; nevertheless the concept is sound, and it gives us a goal to strive for. One thing is clear: The majority of us are now living at a level that is far in excess of a Just World Standard of Living, and so any effort whatsoever to attain greater simplicity is a step in the right direction.

No scientist—nor, to my knowledge, any politician or religious leader—has as yet offered a definitive description of what a Just World Standard of Living might entail. Those of us who are involved with the Simple Living movement, however, have begun to evolve our own rule of thumb. One approach is this: If we are 6 percent of the world's population, then we in the United States should be consuming only 6 percent of the world's resources. If we assume, for the moment, that we are currently consuming thirty percent of the world's resources (a low estimate, as we have seen), then a just standard of living should call for a reduction to one-fifth of what we are now consuming.

Applying the same principle to our energy consumption, we come up with this: Researchers have found that the level of consumption from all sources—coal, wood, gas, petroleum, hydrochemicals—is a very good indicator of the rate of pollution. Measured in terms of pounds of coal equivalent, we in the United States each consume 25,000 pounds per year. Comparable figures for other countries are: the Soviet Union, 10,000 pounds; Italy, 6,500 pounds; Brazil, 1,300 pounds; India, 450 pounds. Overall world consumption per capita is about sixteen percent of our level. Therefore, if we consumed at the current world average, we would consume about one-fifth or less of the energy we do now—in other words, a figure comparable to the one in the paragraph above.

It is important to realize that this energy measure takes all our activities into account—making B-52 bombers as well as producing a television set or heating and cooling our homes. To give a slightly clearer picture, it may be helpful to know that currently 25 percent of our energy goes for transportation, 25 percent goes to heating and cooling residential and commercial establishments, and 32 percent goes into industrial production.

So much for our consumption as United States citizens. Most of us, however, are used to measuring our standard of living in terms of our yearly income. It would, therefore, be helpful if we could come up with an overall figure that would represent something approximating a just standard of living. To my knowledge, no researcher has addressed this problem directly, but the Club of Rome study *The Limits to Growth* has given some of us a starting point for reordering our lives.

The authors project several scenarios, so to speak, of what the world may be like in the future, depending upon the measures taken now. They suggest that only when industrial growth is limited, when the best technological pollution control techniques are utilized, and when population control is achieved—only after all this can we hope for a stable world order, one that will not end in disaster. However, they emphasize that if we begin to make the right decisions now, a stable world order can be achieved. At that leveling-off point, the per capita world income is computed at about $1,800 a year.

Until something more definite is proposed, I would suggest that a per person expenditure of under $2,000 a year is a good rule of thumb for trying to live at a Just World Standard of Living. This figure represents about half the current per capita income in the United States. It is about equal to the per capita income of Europe today. It is far above the income of the average Chinese and yet the indications are that in China today immense strides have been made toward the provision of food and shelter, medical attention, and education for all the people. In other words, $2,000 annually (that is, $8,000 after-tax income for a family of four) affords a decent, sustainable lifestyle that is even quite affluent if it is compared to the situation of most of the people in the world today.

That does not mean that living within such an income will not be fraught with great difficulties for an individual in the United States today. Nevertheless it is a measure that many of us have taken to heart. As we plan out our year and attempt to formulate our budget, we consistently attempt to keep as close to it as possible. We do it out of hope for the social change which is vital for the survival of our society. It is important to recognize, however, that the figure we have arrived at is at present simply a rule of thumb and questions can legitimately be raised about it.

The most important thing to recognize about this, or any other standard computed on the basis of our present economic and productive system, is that the same standard in a rationally redesigned society would unquestionably afford a better lifestyle than it now can. As we have seen, our American system of production and distribution is not designed to be ecological, nor is it geared to a just distribution of resources, nor does it tap our creative potential for designing a rational technology.

Looking into the future, we can see that a $2,000 a year income in a society that had a decent transportation system, a decentralized and creative educational system, a production system that stressed durability and ecological soundness, a health-care system that gave adequate medical attention to all, and so on, would represent a lifestyle that could conceivably be better than one based on two or three times that figure today. Therefore, the most meaningful measure of a Just World Standard of Living would be *one developed as part of a rational world plan of international social and economic redesign.* (We shall have more to say about such a plan in the following chapter.)

At present, however, we do not have that design, though we increasingly possess the potential to develop it. Those of us who are concerned with the Simple Living movement must, therefore, make do with a less sophisticated means of measurement. For many of us the $2,000 a year figure is a good reference point. This usually requires that we live communally and share a common car, television set, washing machine, and so on.

In workshops and in speaking engagements we have been very reluctant to use the $2,000 a year figure because it tends to frighten people. (Remember to multiply by the number of people in your family!) Most middle-class Americans can't imagine how they could possibly live on it; and when we point to our own lifestyle, I'm afraid we seem hopelessly far away from what they could visualize for their own lives. Because of this we have not tried to hold up an objective measurement that would supposedly define "true" simplicity. Moreover, looking into the future we are aware that a redesigned society would solve problems for many more people by providing a variety of living situations, ranging from communal households to village-like clusters and single-family or even single-person dwellings.

What we do suggest to people is that they try to simplify their lives as much as possible. We ask them to sit down with their current budget and see where they might be able to cut back. Then we suggest that in six or twelve months they look at their budget again and try to find further ways to simplify. The most important thing right now is that people should take the first step by declaring themselves ready and willing to live more simply and to reorient their lives and their lifestyles. We are all of us part of a movement that is consciously separating itself from the materialism and the consumer orientation of our society and pointing toward the vision of a new, just world society. As this movement grows and develops, our vision itself will become clearer and more encompassing, and our lifestyles will fall into place.

To help people begin to envision a different lifestyle we have developed an exercise called the Income Game, which we use in workshops. We have found that the game helps "shake loose" old thinking and assumptions and points to a very important underlying principle in this effort to develop a new vision of society. Here is how it works.

Participants are organized in groups of four or five, and each group is given a "group income" for the year. The group must decide how to divide the money among its members for the support of the individuals and of their families for the coming year. Generally we give each group an amount equivalent to one-half their present income, or less. Thus a group composed of a Catholic sister, a single college student, a man representing a family of five, and a woman representing a family of three might have to divide a total of $18,000 between them. We ask the participants to be as realistic as possible and concentrate on their basic needs.

The fascination of this game is twofold: First, it works. Most groups are able to come up with a plan that does provide for their basic needs. Second, it is a lot of fun. Instead of the depression and anxiety that usually accompany a discussion of "cutting back," our participants usually find themselves surprised and exhilarated by their efforts. Starting from scratch and limited by a stated budget, they discover that they are able to simplify their lives dramatically. They begin to see all kinds of new possibilities and have a new sense of financial freedom. We know by experience that had the same groups been asked to have a discussion simply about "how we can simplify," the results might well have been frustration and depression.

There is an important principle illustrated by this game, one we have found to be a key to progress in building a vision for a new society. When people try to build a *new* system from scratch—rather than trying to modify the present system—they make much greater progress in imagining significant change. We have found that workshop participants are able to develop creative and exciting visions of a new society when they are allowed to build from the ground floor. This is important because most people find themselves caught up in the mindset of "how we do things now"—and how we are doing things now is precisely what has got us into trouble.

A JUST NATIONAL PRODUCT

A second concept that has evolved from our efforts to develop a politically aware Simple Living movement is that of a Just National Product. Most people are aware that nations measure their output of goods and services in monetary amounts and that the total of the value "produced" in a year is called the gross national product. We believe that just as there is a *Just World Standard of Living* for individuals, so there is a *Just National Product* for nations. Simply put, this means that every nation can be held to a measurable level of resource consumption that is equitable in terms of overall world needs. Like the concept of Just World Standard of Living, this idea is readily comprehensible, even if at present there might be difficulty in expressing it in terms of quantities and figures. It is easy for most of us to grasp because we have already reached the point of understanding that the globe is a closed system with finite resources and measurable needs.

This growing awareness that we are part of a global system—a "global village," as Marshall MacLuhan has put it—is a tremendously revolutionary concept. There have, of course, been thinkers in the past—poets, philosophers, religious and political leaders—who thought in global terms and saw humankind as one; but today this "radical" concept is just plain common sense to millions of people. This new, and growing, "common sense" is not able to be acquired only by the educated; indeed many reasonably literate children around the world already have it. Its implications are vast; it provides a basic understanding and a simple set of ethical principles capable of remaking our entire planet.

Back before Earth Day, back before the Barry Commoners and Paul Erlichs and thousands of ecology activists began to speak out, back before the Club of Rome report and the United Nations Conference on the Environment, back, perhaps, as little as ten years ago, we Americans could deceive ourselves into thinking that our own growth could continue and that the rest of the world should learn to keep pace with it. Then we could think of our technology, with its production of such an abundance of goods, as a model for humanity. Now we have begun to realize that it is a crime against humanity.

Moreover, there is in the world today a growing consensus that the rich nations are overconsuming the earth's resources and that a new economic order is required if there ever is to be justice—and indeed, if catastrophe is to be averted. Within this new consensus two concepts, that of the Just World Standard of Living and that of the Just National Product (whether expressed in these or other terms), are going to play a leading role in shaping an international movement for global justice. They are already of crucial importance to the Simple Living movement that has begun in the United States (and in Canada and other developed countries in the world), because they provide the theoretical framework that links a simplified lifestyle with a new international order. As the Simple Living movement grows, they must be further developed and refined and made a fundamental part of our efforts toward social change.

Meanwhile, the time has come for us to consider what we have referred to as a rational world plan of international social and economic redesign.

7.   Global Redesign

Imagine, for a moment, that somehow you have been drawn up and out from this planet to a point where you can look at the globe and its people as a whole. If you look at the human panorama from this vantage point, freed from any limitations of family ties, national identification, and ideology, you will see much that doesn't make sense. You will see, for instance, that while millions of people go hungry every day, other millions are supplied with such an abundance of food that their severest health problem is that of weight reduction. You will see that while enough grain is grown to feed sixteen billion people (four times the earth's present population) on a non-meat diet, the citizens of the planet are convinced that there is a shortage of food. You will see that though available world resources are limited, the people of the globe are consuming them as if they were infinite—and, stranger still, some group-ings of the population are consuming, at an ever increasing rate, vast amounts of wood, petrochemicals, metals, and energy in deliberately wasteful processes while others are almost wholly deprived of them. You will see that whereas the earth's surface is vast, multitudes of the world's people are crowding together in large, sprawling cities. And you will see that an enormous proportion of the world's resources and its talents are being used to build battleships, warplanes, and bombs capable of destroying life on the planet.

From this all-seeing vantage point our planet could not

117

seem other than bizarre. With all the needed ingredients for a harmonious and balanced existence—resources, skills, labor power—we are teetering on the edge of self-destruction. If, in the course of your journey into space, the world's national, racial, and ideological divisions had been erased from your mind, you might return and, in your simplicity, proclaim a new "gospel" of sharing, love, and world reorganization. But if you did, you would most likely be ignored, dismissed as a crank, or put away somewhere until you regained your "sanity." That is, until quite lately. Today, as I have suggested in the foregoing chapters, we are being shaken loose from many of our long-held convictions.

I think it is vitally important that more and more people should come to have this kind of global perspective, one in which the world is seen in its entirety and its problems are seen as soluble if they are approached with the intention of securing a just share of our wealth for the whole of humankind. It is as though the earth were a garden needing the skillful attention of a gardener if it is to be restored to its full beauty and yield its potential abundance.

The hope of the Simple Living/Global Justice movement is that increasing numbers of people will come to have the broad vision of the global gardener. The action component of this vision could be called "global redesign," by which I refer to an evolving strategy for reorganizing the planet's social, economic, and political arrangements so that in time a just and harmonious society may take shape. Once a person has this global perspective, particular efforts for change take on a whole new meaning. Whether the activity involved is organizing or a local recycling center or subsistence farming in the country or campaigning for disarmament or lobbying for the internationalization of the oceans' resources—all can, and will, contribute to a broader movement for global redesign. The essential thing is always to keep the planetary perspective at the source of our actions and constantly to remember that our immediate goals should contribute in some way to the fulfillment of the larger needs of our world.

SPECIFIC STRATEGIES

In considering the question of global redesign, one should call to mind the global goal so well expressed in the Shakertown Pledge: that all people shall have access to "the needed resources for their physical, emotional, intellectual, and spiritual growth." As we look at the planet, it is obvious that the physical needs of the world's people should have priority —food to eat, water to drink, freedom from premature death and disease, clothing and shelter. This means a commitment to bringing about a "minimum standard of living" for all the people on this planet.

The Club of Rome, which regards a minimum standard of living as a necessary condition for global harmony, has adopted the phrase "balanced development" to describe their strategy for reaching this goal.[1] What is meant is the pursuit of a global development designed to distribute resources to the areas of greatest need. It would call for the commitment on the part of the "overconsuming" nations to a policy of limiting growth and bringing their use of resources into line with the overall needs of the globe. It would also require that the rich nations should share their technology, their talents, and their material wealth with the poor nations of the world. It is evident that the ideas of a Just World Standard of Living and a Just National Product, which we discussed in the preceding chapter, could be key elements in the effort to formulate a conceptual strategy for balanced development.

For the rich nations balanced development involves the adoption of what has been called a policy of "selective growth." Harvey Seifert, writing in the *Christian Century*, describes it as follows:

Instead of tanks, ornate post offices, and subsidies to build supersonic jets, the direction of the future is toward programs providing more VISTA and Peace Corps volunteers, leaders for youth centers, national park rangers, workers for peace and racial justice, facilitators for growth groups, etc. . . .

More widespread opportunities for aesthetic appreciation could be provided through public funds for symphony orchestras, little theater groups, or folk art galleries, even in smaller communities across the country.

Such a shift in priorities is not properly referred to as a "no growth" or "stationary state" economy. It would restrict production only of those material goods which are wasteful of resources, exploitative of other persons, or destructive of the common environment.[2]

In short, "selective growth" means that the rich nations turn their attention from the production of consumer goods to that of a "service economy." It presupposes that we already have enough of the material goods we need and that future investment should go into teaching, social services, the arts and cleaning up the environment. A country that adopted a policy of selective growth, however, would not freeze its present wealth-distribution patterns. On the contrary, it would have to commit itself to a redistribution of wealth, so that all of its people would be enjoying a comfortable lifestyle.

For the poor countries, balanced growth would mean that national and regional development stagies would stress self-sufficiency and "appropriate technology." "Appropriate technology" means that industrial production and the introduction of machinery and tools would be geared to a strategy which attempts to raise the living standard of all the people, rather than the present pattern of overdeveloping one sector at the expense of others. Such a strategy would abandon the attempts to build miniature Japans throughout the developing world and concentrate instead on developing the skills and resources of the people. As a native group in Botswana declared:

We can make doors and doorframes from our own timber, and we can even make glass by melting bottles in furnaces. We can make windmills for our wells. We can all learn to thatch. All of us can learn improved methods of gardening using very little water. . . . We can grow sunflower and groundnuts to produce cooking oil, and cotton from which we can make rough cloth. . . . If we work together in this way, we will find that each one has work and that we shall be able to obtain by working together most of those things we want to buy from the shops but cannot because we have no money.[3]

Some people may fear that the goal of "balanced development," as outlined above, means that the poorer countries will be relegated to a kind of second-class citizenship, where they content themselves with a per capita living standard of, say, $500 per year, while the rich world continues at $3,000 per capita. This is certainly not my goal or the goal of the people I am working with. Our goal is the equitable distribution of the world's resources, so that in time every citizen of the planet will enjoy a decent and roughly comparable standard of living.

Since this standard of living must be enjoyed within the limits set by the ecosphere, it may well be that the standard of living and the lifestyle of the future world citizen will be closer to the model of self-sufficiency and subsistence than some of us might imagine. Perhaps a balanced and just world society will contain an artful and satisfying combination of small, face-to-face production (like that which the Botswana group envisions, and very similar to the vision of our own "back to the land" movement) and carefully selected "high technology" to meet other needs (continued use of computers, for example, and of communications technology).

Whatever mixture of technology our society finally decides upon, it seems clear to me that if we were to bend our efforts in a global program of reconstruction, we could achieve our goal of physical well-being and ecological balance in thirty years or less. This means that many of us living today could see in our own lifetimes the realization of humankind's age-old quest for material well-being.

In the pages that follow, I shall try to give a more detailed picture of the techniques and substrategies that are available now and could be used to help us reach our goal.

THE RICH NATIONS

What strategies will the rich nations need to follow if they are to play their part in the formation of a just global society? What will they have to give up? What will they gain? Here I will focus on the consideration of these questions with regard to the United States economy, hoping that such a discussion will outline an approach that can be taken to all developed economies.

Three considerations must guide any plan for reorganizing

the United States economy: (1) our economic and production system must function within the limits of our environment; (2) our production and distribution system should be geared to provide for the basic needs of all our people; (3) our consumption level should be such that we are not taking more than our fair share of the world's resources and we should also be willing to share our resources and skills with people who need them.

The policy implications of these principles are:

First, that we must *evolve and implement a national plan for putting our production on an ecologically sound basis.* According to Barry Commoner:

This will require the development of major new technologies, including: systems to return sewage and garbage directly to the soil; the replacement of many synthetic materials by natural ones; the reversal of the present trend to retire land from cultivation and to elevate the yield per acre by heavy fertilization; replacement of synthetic pesticides, as rapidly as possible, by biological ones; the discouragement of power-consuming industries; the development of land transport that operates with maximum fuel efficiency at low combustion temperatures and with minimal land use; essentially complete containment and reclamation of wastes from combustion processes, smelting, and chemical operations (smokestacks must become rarities); essentially complete recycling of all reusable metal, glass, and paper products; ecologically sound planning to govern land use, including urban areas.[4]

Dr. Commoner estimates that it would cost about $600 billion to make this conversion over a twenty-five year period. The best system, he says, would be the one that is closest to natural processes and uses natural materials rather than synthetic ones. In time, he envisions a global industrial system in which factories are located near the sites of their materials and produce with minimal polluting. Any proposal for new technology would first have to be screened for its environmental impact, and only if it passed the test would it be utilized.

The second policy implication is that we must *evolve and implement a national plan that gears our production to meeting the basic needs of our people.* This means that we must focus our energy on meeting the needs of our population for food, housing, and education and on providing each and every person with a minimum, decent standard of living. Since we must do this within a framework of limited resources and ecological considerations, we obviously must make durability, repairability, and multiple use the hallmarks of our system. As I have suggested, our present consumer goods system is incredibly wasteful. Were we to produce the best goods possible, with the most natural materials and using the most creative engineering and design, we might very well find that we could provide our people with a living standard as good as, or better than, that currently enjoyed in this country, and do so without overtaxing the world's resources.

Third, we must *reorganize our system so that all people are provided with opportunities for utilizing their creative and productive talents.* Meaningful occupation is probably a basic need of humankind along with food, clothing, and shelter. Human beings deteriorate without purposeful employment of their talents, and the best society will be organized so that human capacities do not go to waste. Millions of people in this country are at present unemployed or underemployed—and so also are hundreds of millions throughout the world. Our nation and our globe cannot afford such a loss—there are simply too many things that need to be done. Community and agricultural development, industrial conversion and new plant development along ecological lines, literacy training and education at all levels, social and health needs, environmental reclamation, and pioneering research into meeting the present and future needs of humankind—all these are needs which our globe has today.

If we can be utopian and look to a time in the not too distant future when the basic human needs are met, then the social encouragement of meaningful employment will be even more important. Should we ever reach a point where human beings can devote the greatest part of their time to doing what they want to do rather than what they *have* to do, we will need even more inventive educators and social programs to help people discover and develop their creative talents.

This does not necessarily mean that our government would have to provide a "job" for everyone. An alternate policy would be the guarantee of an annual income for each individual, or the guarantee of certain basic necessities of life. Once that security was established, we could have a national policy of encouraging volunteer work in the many fields of human endeavor that provide services necessary to society. Today volunteer work is flourishing in this country, whether in education, health care, aid to the disabled, or service abroad. It seems to me very probable that, with the establishment of a guaranteed standard of living, voluntary service might become the norm in the society of the future. Difficult, dirty, dangerous, or emotionally taxing jobs could be apportioned on the basis of higher wages or through a national system of required service for a fixed period of years.

A fourth policy implication is that the United States would be called upon to commit itself and its resources to the implementation of an *international plan of reconstruction and development*. Such a plan could be drawn up by the United Nations or some other international body. (In fact, similar plans have already been drawn up, but they have not been inspired by ecological principles of redesign, and even their limited objectives for aid have not been met by the United States and other participating nations.) This would mean our committing a generous portion of our resources and our human talents to a global effort for development. It would involve our participation in a plan that would gradually loosen our hold on the disproportionate share of the world's resources we now have and mandate the sharing of our abundance with others (food immediately comes to mind). In addition we would participate in international "technology pools" to make the latest techniques available to developing nations (in marked contrast to our present policy whereby corporations keep our best technology for themselves or sell it at exorbitant rates).

Needless to say, a United States commitment to assist genuine development in the poorer nations would mean the end of our policy of undermining governments whose domestic economic policies pose a threat to our corporations. It would mean shifting our support from repressive regimes to those sincerely attempting to help all their people.

NEW VISION

It is unlikely that the people of the United States, or of any other wealthy country, would be willing to participate in the kind of national reorganization we are proposing unless there were compelling reasons to do so. Much as we might wish that love of neighbor could be the inspiration of such changes, it is improbable that this sentiment will be sufficiently strong and broadly diffused to serve the purpose. What is needed is the *vision of a new society* that is in *right relation to global realities* and hence offers greater possibilities even for the developed nations than the continuance of our present system. I believe that the projection of such a vision is not only possible and practicable but urgently necessary. The time has come for Americans, and likewise people around the world, to begin in earnest to develop it.

During the workshops that some of us in the Simple Living/ Global Justice movement have conducted, we have often included a time when we asked people to formulate their own vision of what a good society would be like. Sometimes we do a "vision gallery" in which we ask participants to express their concept of the new society in a drawing. These are then displayed for all to see.

Another activity we have developed is the "island exercise," whose purpose is to discover what level of technology people would be satisfied with. It goes like this: We ask the participants to close their eyes and imagine they are alone on an island. We say that the island has no dangerous animals, has plenty of water and plenty to eat year round in the form of fruits and wild nuts and grains, and is large enough for a lifetime of exploration. "What would you do there?" we ask them. After allowing some time for silent exploration of their island and its possibilities, we suggest that they can bring as many of their friends along as they desire. When they have had time to include that in their fantasies, we say: "Now imagine that you and your friends are gathered for a meeting. The purpose is to decide what level of technology you want to import to the island. You can bring in anything you like: electricity, steel tools, stereos, washing machines, horses and buggies, a printing press. Just remember that whatever technology you import you will have to maintain."

Surprisingly, we found that most people want to bring in almost nothing and are in fact content to live more or less at a subsistence level. Nobody in our groups has wanted nuclear power, computers, or submarines. But they haven't wanted televisions, hair dryers, or washing machines either. So far, very few have wanted even electricity.

It is fascinating to speculate on this. Can it be that the people who have the most technologically advanced civilization in the world would just as soon give it all up? Does the prospect of leisure time, security, and liberation from the requirements of an advanced industrial society provide such an attractive picture that our people might be willing to forego the fruits of the consumer goods industry—even forego electricity?

It may well be that our tests have involved only an atypical minority (after all, who would come to a Simple Living workshop, anyway?); or perhaps people's fantasies don't really tell you much about their realistic needs and actual behavior. But I doubt that that is the case. My own suspicion is that if we tried this exercise with a variety of American groups we would get surprisingly similar results. In any event, I think that except for the natural-born Robinson Crusoes we would find that most people would be content to live within a far less technologically complicated society than we now have. The pastoral image, the vision of living in a garden paradise, is a very powerful archetype in the human psyche, one that is recurrent in literature and art. It seems to me that it may very well be more than a romantic throwback to some idealized "good old days"; rather, it may be a strong vision in the collective unconscious, embodying the wisdom and joy derived from living in harmony with nature instead of trying to despoil it.

William Morris thought so too. Artist, poet, gentleman, revolutionary, he was offended by the Victorian literature that described itself as "utopian." The most particular object of his ire was Edward Bellamy's *Looking Backward,* an American novel set in Boston in the year 2000. Bellamy's utopia was the forerunner of our present-day stereotypes of this genre —superurban, supertechnological. Living in this ideal Boston is like living inside a machine. Encased in concrete, glass, and metal tubing, the resident had every need met by mechanical means—both food and music were piped in. Citizens worked in an "industrial army" in which the length of service was a mere twenty years. After that, one could retire and turn to enjoying the full fruits of modern civilization.

Morris's own utopian novel, *News from Nowhere,* presents a total contrast to Bellamy's views. Morris's London of the future, unlike Bellamy's Boston, was a green and pleasant town. Most of its factories were gone and the river was clean. The iron bridges that once spanned the Thames had been replaced by bridges built of stone (because the people like them better).

This society of Morris's vision has much in common with that of medieval England, or indeed eighteenth-century America. Its people travel on horseback or on foot. It has no compulsory education. (For, as one citizen remarks: "The information lies ready to each one's hand when his own inclinations impel him to seek it. In this as in other matters we have become wealthy; we can afford to give ourselves time to grow.")[5] It is primarily an agricultural, village society; technology is used only for the few tasks one wishes to perform manually. There is no money—people make things and give them to one another. All socially necessary work is performed out of pleasure rather than necessity. People trade jobs frequently and tasks like harvesting are turned into celebrations and sport.

William Morris believed that most of the impedimenta of "modern society" were brought along by industrial capitalism and that if people were given a choice, they would choose a simpler, face-to-face society. For Morris, Bellamy's utopia was simply the logical extension of the capitalist system—a socialist state that was like an immense monopoly, one for which everyone worked. Better, Morris thought, to have a simpler society in which necessary work was minimized and nature respected.

Morris's work presaged our own "back to the land" movement of the 1960s and 1970s. Readers will recognize, in my short account of his thought, the very ideas and ideals that motivate so many of the young and not so young people who today have forsaken the dubious pleasures of urban civilization and returned to the countryside. Today it is widely felt that just such a detechnologized, decentralized society is the goal we should be aiming for in our efforts to reconstruct the planet.

For example, the *Blueprint for Survival* put together by the editors of the British magazine *The Ecologist,* calls for a radically decentralized economy and body politic. It envisions a society consisting of villages and small towns whose food is supplied from the surrounding neighborhood and whose manufactured goods are also locally derived. It envisions neighborhoods of 500 people, communities of 5,000, and regions of 500,000. It is through these small settlements rather than through nation-states and urban conglomerates that the process of decision-making essential to the conduct of government flows. In these communities people could interact with one another in a meaningful way. In addition to the increased manageability of the political process and the advantages of closer and more genuine personal relations between neighbors, the planners point to the ecological dimension:

To deploy a population in small towns and villages is to reduce to the minimum its impact on the environment. This is because the actual urban superstructure required per inhabitant goes up radically as the size of the town increases beyond a certain point. For example, the per capita cost of high-rise apartment buildings is much greater than that of ordinary houses; and the cost of roads and other transportation routes increases with the number of commuters carried. Similarly, the per capita expenditure on facilities such as those for distributing food and removing waste is much higher in cities than in small towns and villages.[6]

In their book *Communitas,* American planners Paul and Percival Goodman have suggested that a national plan calling for the creation of medium-sized towns (100,000 or less) would be wholly feasible.[7] They estimate that a subsistence economy providing food, shelter, medical services, transportation, and clothing and based on a decentralized industrial structure would require only about 10 percent of the production capacity we now utilize. In such a subsistence economy, they calculate that on the average people would have to work only for six or seven years of their life in order to justify the allotment of a full share in the benefits of society.[8]

Perhaps the foregoing examples of what is being worked out in the area of social planning will, for the moment, suffice to show that it is entirely possible to envision a radically altered social and economic structure that might be attractive to the majority of our people and would, at the same time, be in harmony with our environment. These are designs that might likewise be applied to the needs of others among the world's peoples. In the following pages, I will explore some of the ideas and the technologies that may help to transform the poorer nations; and in this presentation will be seen many techniques and models that might inspire us in the attempt to rethink the outlines of our own society.

TECHNOLOGY AND DEVELOPMENT
IN THE POOR LANDS

As we have seen, one of the most serious problems developing countries have had to face is the pressure to adopt a model of growth patterned after the industrial development of Europe and the United States. This pressure comes from the Western-oriented, educated elite in many of these countries, but it has also come from the planners who accompany the developed countries' foreign aid.

It will be recalled that the trouble with such a model has been the creation of the following problems: (1) It has established an ideal of industrial development and mass consumption often ecologically unsound in the country involved; (2) it has meant in most instances the continued underdevelopment of the rural sector of the country's economy, the progressive enrichment of the national elite, and the complexification and choking overpopulation of major cities; and (3) it has prevented the development of a sound economy owing to the prohibitive difficulties underdeveloped nations experience in placing finished industrial goods in the highly competitive international market unless they are willing to be subservient to large corporations and powerful nations.

In recent years a number of voices have been raised to challenge this model of development. Foremost in this area of criticism is Dr. E. F. Schumacher, formerly chief economist for the National Coal Board of Great Britain and currently active in spreading a new vision of economic development. In his book *Small Is Beautiful,* Schumacher follows Gandhi in urging an emphasis on "production by the masses" rather than "mass production" for the people of the developing countries:

> The system of *mass production,* based on sophisticated, highly capital-intensive, high energy-input dependent, and human labour-saving technology, presupposes that you are already rich, for a great deal of capital investment is needed to establish one single workplace. The system of *production by the masses* mobilizes the priceless resources which are possessed of all human beings, their clever brains and skillful hands, *and supports them with first-class tools.* . . . The technology of *production by the masses,* making use of the best of modern knowledge and experience, is conducive to decentralization, compatible with the laws of ecology, gentle in its use of scarce resources, and designed to serve the human person instead of making him the servant of machines. I have named it *intermediate technology* to signify that it is vastly superior to the primitive technology of bygone ages but at the same time simpler, cheaper, and freer than the supertechnology of the rich.[9]

"Intermediate Technology" envisions a pattern of widespread and organic growth in which the entire populace participates. It advocates a steady push from the bottom, rather than the rapid elevation of one sector from which benefits for the masses are supposed to "trickle down." It tries to use the native skills of the people, the national materials that are present, and it builds on the real and immediate needs of the populace (water, housing, food, simple transportation, basic education) rather than on the needs of an affluent elite (automobiles, office buildings, universities, luxury goods).

Dr. Schumacher has been instrumental in forming a group in England that advocates and assists this approach; it is called the Intermediate Technology Development Group. This organization has been able to tap the resources of experts in industry, textiles, food, health, water, power and other developmental areas and utilize their skills in designing plans and equipment for use in the scheme of "production by the masses." It is their hope that in time most international economic and development aid will be directed more toward the Intermediate Technology approach. Already Germany has announced the formation of an Intermediate Technology advisory group to assist its aid program.

Examples of Intermediate Technology and of its potential are easily found. The British group, for example, was able to help Zambia develop a machine that made egg cartons for farmers by pulping wastepaper. Under ordinary large-scale design, the most efficient machine would have to produce one million cartons a month in order to be economical. The redesigned equipment is economical at a production level of one million cartons a year.[10] Another example, cited by both Schumacher and Papanek, is a brick-making machine:

This simple device is used as follows: mud or earth is packed into a brick-shaped receptacle, a large lever is pulled down, and a perfect "rammed earth" brick results. This apparatus permits people to "manufacture" bricks at their own speed—500,000 a day or two a week. Out of these bricks schools, homes, and hospitals have been built all over South America and the rest of the Third World.[11]

Other examples are the eight-dollar television set that could be used for village educational programming, and the six-dollar refrigerator that can be used for storage of goods for market. Both of these designs by Victor Papanek and his coworkers are capable of local manufacture with Intermediate Technology methods. Papanek's nine-cent radio can be made by any person who possesses the few mechanical parts, a tin can, and some fuel source like cow dung.

Most planners and designers, according to Papanek, are working on the "needs" of the world's affluent minority, while the poor majority—some 2,300,000,000 people—have needs that are systematically ignored. For example, there is a need for a simple pipe-making machine, similar to the brick-making machine, which could be used by local people and the pipe from which could be instrumental in insuring an adequate village water supply. There is a need for a multipurpose land vehicle capable of carrying loads over rough terrain and powered in a nonpolluting fashion. There is a need for simple equipment and procedures that can be used to preserve crops once harvested. There is a need for mobile educational and health teams that can service rural areas and train people in elementary health care and sanitation. To this list can be added a more general one drawn up by the Club of Rome. It applies to developed and developing countries alike:

> New methods of waste collection, to decrease pollution and make discarded material available for recycling
> More efficient techniques for recycling, to reduce rates of resource depletion
> Better product design to increase product lifetime and promote easy repair
> Harnessing solar energy, the most pollution-free power source
> Developing methods of natural pest control
> Medical advances that would decrease the death rate
> Contraceptive advances that would facilitate the equalization of the birth rate with the decreasing death rate[12]

The Chinese Model

The development strategy of the People's Republic of China provides a good example of the workings of an Intermediate Technology approach. When the Chinese Civil War ended in 1949, the new government found itself faced with the problems presented by a ravaged land, limited resources, and an immense population. The development strategy that the Chinese pursued in these circumstances is chronicled by British economists E.L. Wheelwright and Bruce McFarlane in their book *The Chinese Road to Socialism.*

The Chinese leadership decided upon a plan that stressed balanced industrial and agricultural development and attempted to avail itself of the tremendous human resources that were at hand. They also decided to respect the agrarian basis of Chinese society, and thus tried to bring revolutionary production methods to the farmlands. Peasants and farmers were organized collectively, either in cooperatives or communes ranging from around five thousand to a hundred thousand members. A commune is really a productive and administrative unit and is composed of numerous villages. This basic production unit was responsible for the improvement of the land, irrigation, the growing of crops for local consumption and for export. It was also responsible for meeting the educational, social, and health needs of its members. Like the kibbutz in Israel, the commune was to be primarily a self-supporting unit. In addition to agriculture, communes were aided and encouraged to develop both light industry and some more heavily mechanized industry in the locale. The making of clothing, shoes, bicycles, steel tools, medicines, wood products, and so on, came to be part of the productive capacity of these rural collectives.

The Chinese deliberately avoided concentration of their industrial capacity in a few major production centers, not only with the idea of speading the skills and the economic opportunity but also with the idea of a more decentralized approach to military defense. Small and medium-sized plants were established in provincial areas and encouraged to draw their material from local sources. Workers were encouraged to contribute whatever innovations and inventions they could to the process, and communes were urged to place themselves on as self-sufficient a basis as possible.[13]

It is helpful and instructive to contrast China with a country that has "successfully" pursued the industrial production/international market model, namely Brazil. As we saw in an earlier chapter, while American economists call its 10 percent annual growth in gross national product an "economic miracle," millions of peasants in the northeast region of Brazil go without the basic necessities of life, work under conditions of semiserfdom, and are found flooding the cities, looking for jobs and for food.[14] The testimony of thousands of outsiders who have visited China is to the effect that the people are well-fed, have adequate health care and educa-

tional opportunities, and are actively engaged in the process
of their country's development.

The Population Question

Many people tend to regard the population question as the
crucial problem the world faces today. As I have suggested in
my opening chapters, the threat posed by rich-world overconsumption and pollution is far greater and much more
immediate than the population growth of underdeveloped
countries. Nevertheless, no solution to the world's problems
will be complete—or stable—unless population growth is reduced and finally halted.

The essential ingredient for stabilizing population growth,
however, is not new technology or sophisticated distribution
techniques. The most important ingredient is *motivation*.
Unless families in developing countries *want* to have fewer
children, population control will be an impossibility.

When we of the Western world look at countries like India
and Indonesia, it seems obvious to us that poor families
should recognize that it is in their own best interest to have
fewer children. But we are wrong. Until needed social and
economic reforms are made, it makes sense for individual
families to keep having more children. As one report on the
failure of a birth control program in India concludes:

An overwhelming majority of the people in Khanna Study have a large
number of children because they *want* larger families. More important, they
want them because they *need* them.

The majority of people in Manupur need children because they are poor.
The work of staying alive is hard work—and they cannot afford to buy
labour-saving machines or to pay other people for the help they need.

From a very early age, the children of Manupur make a vital contribution
to the family well-being. They look after cattle; they help with sowing crops,
weeding and harvesting; they bring in the families' water supply and take
the food out to the fields at midday . . . ; they help with the household
jobs—sewing, cleaning, cooking, and washing.

What is more, children are often the only "insurance" for the poor.
Without children, there is no help or support in illness or old age—and
illness is frequent and old age can begin at forty.[15]

The key to a solution of the population problem is the general economic betterment of the poor. When the basic necessities of life and security for old age are assured, when life is no longer a pitiless struggle for survival in which every hand is needed, perhaps families will no longer feel that they need great numbers of children. Furthermore, when literacy has spread, when employment is available for men and women, when leisure time and creative activity have become a real possibility for all the people in a society, then the economic significance of large numbers of children will have changed: from being a safeguard against insecurity they will have become a responsibility with respect to the parents' freedom and cultural advancement.

An examination of comparative figures from South Korea and Brazil, drawn from data supplied by the Overseas Development Council, Washington, D.C., proves to be very instructive in this regard (table 6).

What these data suggest—and they are supported by information from Taiwan and China—is that *when development is*

Table 6
COMPARATIVE DATA: SOUTH KOREA AND BRAZIL

	South Korea	Brazil
Population growth rates		
1958	3.0%	3.0%
1964	2.7%	2.9%
1971	2.0%	2.8%
Income per capita (1971)	$280	$395
GNP growth rates (1960s)	9.0%	6.0%
Ratio of income, richest 20% to poorest 20%	5 to 1	25 to 1
Joblessness	negligible	serious
Effective land reform	yes	no

Source: Data supplied by Overseas Development Council, Washington, D.C.

spread out to the general population, the birth rate begins to take care of itself. Witness the fact that while Brazil's gross national product per capita is much higher than South Korea's ($395 compared to $280), South Korea's national income is more evenly distrubuted (5 to 1 as opposed to 25 to 1!). Another striking figure: South Korea's infant mortality rate (deaths per 1,000 births) is 41, while Brazil's is 94. This points to another interesting fact about development and population: at first, infant health-care improvement leads to larger families; but as parents become more confident that their children will survive, the number they have declines.

Therefore, it is not necessary to introduce draconian measures for forced birth control into a workable plan for global redesign: population limitation will occur voluntarily once the necessary material base for a secure life has been provided.

PRINCIPLES OF
BALANCED WORLD DEVELOPMENT

The tremendous task of global redesign can be accomplished only if there is a basic acceptance of certain operating principles to guide our efforts. On a pragmatic level, these principles are very simple: We must design a system which (1) is in harmony with the ecosphere; (2) provides a decent life for all the world's people; and (3) respects individual rights and freedom of worship and information, in order that each person's opportunity for emotional, intellectual, and spiritual growth may be maximized.

Many students of the world situation argue that if we are ever going to make the development of a new global society based on these principles a reality, humankind must have a "global ethic" to guide it. Such an ethic, they feel, must be one which combines love of neighbor, love for future generations and consideration for their well-being, and respect for the natural processes of the planet.[16] Central to it will be the acceptance of the principle that enough is enough: in other words, that the affluent nations and their people must realize that their reckless pursuit of material gain is plundering the earth and agree to limit their consumption with a view to the equitable sharing of the world's resources.

But of course there are several problems with respect to this ethic that enough is enough; they have emerged in our discussions in the foregoing chapters. The developed economies, as we have seen, are dependent for their well-being on continuing "growth," and there is a widespread fear that if it should cease, the economies would collapse. Moreover, the members of these societies have been induced to define well-being—indeed, status—in terms of their material consumption. Madison Avenue has done its job well; most people have learned to live by and for the goods they consume, and for many their identity as persons has been shaped by their possessions. It will not be easy to alter this materialistic orientation, though there are signs that recent years have been productive of a more widespread distrust of our affluent society than was once the case.

When people like Lewis Mumford and Robert Heilbroner consider the human prospect, they come to one shared conclusion: unless humankind is able to develop a new vision of the world and of what life could be like, we are in deep trouble. Thus they turn, almost in desperation, to the hope that a spiritual awakening of major proportions may come to humankind. To Heilbroner, unless people turn from their materialism and begin to cultivate and enjoy the "inner states" of being, there is little hope.[17] Mumford speaks of a "human awakening" in which God rises up again in "the human soul."[18] We will need, he says, to attain to a new vision of what society can be; and we must learn to value and to seek "balance, wholeness, completeness," and "continuous interplay between the inner and the outer, the subjective and the objective. . . ."[19]

E.F. Schumacher is convinced that the world must learn to accept the fundamental truths of the great world religions, particularly their teaching with regard to seeking first the spiritual kingdom; humankind would profit by the Buddhist doctrine of "Right Livelihood" and the cardinal Christian virtues of *prudentia, justitia, fortitudo,* and *temperantia.*[20]

For Christians the conclusions of these scholars, who are looking thoughtfully upon what they regard as the deepening crisis in present-day society, should come as an affirmation of the central tenet of our faith: love. We should see in them the validation of Christ's teaching with regard to seeking first the kingdom of God, with regard to the impossibility of serving God and mammon. Surely, we should be saying to ourselves, our faith provides the basis for the "new ethic" necessary to save the world. But here is the irony: The developed nations, the wealthy nations engaged in despoiling the world of its resources, are by and large precisely those that have historically constituted Christendom or are regarded as mainly Christian in their derivation. And within these nations, are the Christian churches witnessing to the injunction against laying up treasures here on earth, or are they pioneering in the development of a global ethic of sharing? The answer, I say with regret, must be for the most part no.

And thus the challenge: Are we capable of rediscovering the radical message of the gospel and bringing it to bear on the present world situation? Can we revive and strengthen in our own lives, in the life of our churches and the life of our nation, the principles of our Christian witness? And can we work with and respect people of other faiths, so that together we can forge a universal ethic for humankind?

What the new vision of the world will call for is this: Disengaging ourselves from what are purely matters of national self-interest and political ideology, we shall look at the world rather as God might, seeing humankind in its totality and allowing our love, our compassion, and our creative intelligence to reach out to embrace it—and beyond humankind, the animals, plants, and natural forces belonging to the ecosphere. With our heads in the clouds—in the vision God grants us—we will have to "walk" on the ground; that is, to make our vision relevant and practical. This is quite an undertaking, given our record.

In the next section of this book, I shall take a close look at the Christian churches, particularly with respect to their role in present-day society. Only after we have taken stock of our present resources, our limitations, and our strengths can we attempt to evaluate the possibilities of a Christian response to the global crisis. Are we, as some fear, destined to be part of the problem or, as others hope, part of the solution?

NOTES

1. Mihajlo Mesarovic and Eduard Pestel, eds., *Mankind at the Turning Point,* The Second Report to the Club of Rome (New York: Dutton, 1974), p. 127.

2. "Stagflation and the Church," February 19, 1975.

3. John V. Taylor, *Enough Is Enough,* p. 92.

4. *The Closing Circle,* pp. 282–283.

5. *Three Works by William Morris* (New York: International Publishers, 1968), p. 246.

6. P. 40.

7. New York: Vintage, 1960.

8. Ibid., pp. 191-201.

9. P. 145.

10. Taylor, *Enough Is Enough,* p.89.

11. Papanek, *Design for the Real World,* p. 88.

12. Meadows et al., *The Limits to Growth,* p. 182.

13. E.L. Wheelwright and Bruce McFarlane, *The Chinese Road to Socialism* (New York: Monthly Review Press, 1970).

14. See Paul Gallet, *Freedom to Starve* (Baltimore: Penguin, 1967); see also Francisco Juliao, *Cambao–The Yoke* (Baltimore: Penguin, 1972).

15. *The New Internationalist,* October 1974.

16. See Mesarovic and Pestel, *Mankind at the Turning Point,* p. 147; Editors of *The Ecologist, Blueprint for Survival,* pp. 18–19; Schumacher, *Small Is Beautiful,* pp. 278–79.

17. *An Inquiry into the Human Prospect* (New York: Norton, 1974), p. 140.

18. *The Pentagon of Power* (New York: Harcourt, 1964), p. 413.

19. Ibid., p. 396.

20. Schumacher, *Small Is Beautiful,* pp. 278–281.

III. A LOOK AT
THE CHURCH

"Action on behalf of justice and participation in the transformation of the world fully appear to us as a constitutive dimension of the preaching of the Gospel, or in other words, of the Church's mission for the redemption of the human race and its liberation from every oppressive situation. While the Church is bound to give witness to justice, she recognizes that anyone who ventures to speak to people about justice must first be just in their eyes."

—JUSTICE IN THE WORLD, STATEMENT
BY THE SYNOD OF BISHOPS, ROME, 1971

8. The Churches' Wealth

"The Church is obliged to live and administer its own goods in such a way that the Gospel is proclaimed to the poor. If instead the Church appears to be among the rich and powerful of this world, its credibility is diminished."

—1971 ROMAN SYNOD OF BISHOPS

Item: The total institutional wealth of all churches and religious organizations in the United States is reliably estimated at $134.3 billion. The annual cash flow through Christian religious institutions is $21 billion.[1]

Item: In 1962 St. Mary's Roman Catholic Cathedral in San Francisco burned to the ground. The diocese quickly launched a $15 million drive to build a new $6 million cathedral, a seminary, a home for the aged, and three new high schools. A local chapter of the Catholic Interracial Council conducted a campaign to have $1 million of the total raised given over to projects to help the Bay area poor. They were turned down.[2]

Item: A Baptist church structure that was recently completed in Dallas, Texas, boasts a seven-story parking and recreation building that contains a skating rink, gymnasium, and four bowling lanes.[3]

Item: The Anglican Cathedral of Christ the King was completed in Liverpool, England, at a cost of 4 million pounds ($12 million). It features a 340-foot crown, "containing 12,000 square feet of colored glass (more than any other cathedral in the world, including Chartres)."[4]

Item: By 1968 the Episcopal National Cathedral in Washington had cost $30 million. Estimates were that it would require another $20 million to complete.[5]

If there is anything about the Christian church that is clear to religious and nonreligious alike, it is that some nineteen hundred and seventy years after the birth of its founder it is a phenomenally wealthy institution. Trying to make it appear otherwise is a little like trying to hide an elephant in a telephone booth.

"The Catholic Church," says Fr. Richard Ginder, a nationally syndicated columnist, "must be the biggest corporation in the United States. We have a branch office in every neighborhood. Our assets and real estate holdings must exceed those of Standard Oil, AT&T, and U. S. Steel combined."[6] Granting that there are exceptions—the small denominations with unpaid clergy, the groups whose "establishment" consists in prayer meetings in people's homes—by and large the Christian church, the church dedicated to the man who praised poverty and adjured his followers to carry only one cloak and one pair of sandals, is a consciously and deliberately luxurious institution in most of its home territories today. Costly cathedrals with their treasures of art, architecturally exciting churches, well-appointed national headquarters, slick promotional literature, and executives who in their jet travel are difficult to distinguish from those of large corporations—all these are signs of the ease and affluence of the twentieth-century church.

As one close observer of the American religious scene has put it:

Today the parish norm for American Protestants, Roman Catholics, and Jews alike is indeed the upholstered, in many instances the air-conditioned, pew. And few sophisticated church trustees regard their parishes as adequately appointed if limited to a church sanctuary, Sunday School group, and a parsonage. The fashionable parish, Protestant or Catholic, fundamentalist or "modernist," also must—and usually does—have at least a "Christian Education wing," a banquet and recreation complex, an auxiliary chapel, one or more hard-surfaced parking lots, multiple parsonages for its multi-member ministerial staff, a vehicle fleet, and a woods-and-water recreation camp.[7]

"Adapt yourself no longer to the pattern of this present world," advises Paul in his letter to the Romans, "but let your minds be remade and your whole nature thus transformed." The "mind remade" that has shaped the style of the church in America is the mind of the affluent booster, the person who equates size and comfort with value, and who apparently thinks that God and God's friends need fairly luxurious points of contact to keep the whole thing going.

I will never forget how startled I was when, after addressing a Presbyterian congregation located in a large and airy stone building in the Delaware suburbs, I learned that they had moved from their old (and perfectly adequate) building to a new brick structure right next to the country club. The cost of this new edifice: one million dollars. Nor will the impression soon fade of my recent visit to the headquarters of a major Protestant denomination located in the Philadelphia suburbs. In this modern, architecturally interesting, air-conditioned building, I would have found it very difficult to guess what these well-nourished, well-dressed employees were so busy about had I not already known. Conformed to the world? Yes, indeed. It could have been the headquarters of any major multinational corporation, for all its style of life gave away.

The church has gone the way of its culture. Surrounded by affluence, it has let itself slide into a very affluent lifestyle, sometimes even arguing that this is the only way in which it will be taken seriously.

And thus the church finds itself in a very awkward position when the topic turns to global justice. A perfect example was afforded recently by a national "consultation" on global justice. One hundred Roman Catholic, Protestant, and Jewish leaders gathered in a posh ski resort cum conference center in Aspen, Colorado. There, amidst the lavish surroundings, the cocktail parties, the elegant meals served by French chefs, the participants considered the topic at hand. And the topic, of course, was global justice and the inequities of our planetary distribution system.

Speaker after speaker led the conferees through the litany about starving children, lowered foreign aid appropriations, the need for greater sharing, and so on. In the end they agreed on a few resolutions and recommendations. Then they all went to the airport, got on their jets, and flew off to other equally important meetings in various parts of the world.

Just before they left, they adopted the reports of their committees. One of the reports endorsed the Shakertown Pledge!

HOW RICH IS THE CHURCH, ANYWAY?

It is not easy to get an accurate estimate of church wealth in the United States. There is no central body in the Roman Catholic hierarchy that collects such data, and among the Protestants there is a considerable diversity of accounting practices (including a number of denominations who do not publish their figures). The best and most reliable estimate has been calculated by Martin A. Larson and Stanley Lowell and is reported in their book *The Churches: Their Riches, Revenues, and Immunities.* Larson and Lowell had a compelling reason for gathering their statistics: They believe that church property should be taxed. The researchers therefore set out to determine as accurately as possible just how much wealth they were dealing with and how much was being lost to local, state, and national coffers in potential taxes each year. (Their estimate: $2.22 billion in property taxes alone.[8] And if business income and capital gains on gifts and bequests were also taxed, that would add another $5 billion a year.[9])

The researchers obtained their gross figures by focusing on the tax records for ten United States cities. By a careful analysis of the public records plus the financial reports put out by some dioceses and denominations, they were able to compute total religious wealth (including Jewish institutions) for some of the following locations: Buffalo, New York, $230 million; Washington, D.C., $627 million; Denver, Colorado, $216 million; Boston, Massachusetts, $453 million.

They then took these figures and multiplied them by a predetermined factor that was calculated to determine the total religious property value in the country. Their result: an estimate that religious institutions have $101.4 billion tied up in property (an estimated 7.5 percent of which represents Jewish institutions).[10] Estimates of total religious holdings of stocks, bonds, and commercial real estate were totalled at $20 billion.[11] Remaining religious wealth would consist of art objects, teaching equipment, books, automobiles, and so on.

Putting it all together, here is the authors' balance sheet of the churches (table 7).

Table 7
BALANCE SHEET OF THE CHURCHES

CHURCH INCOME	Protestant	Catholic
Annual voluntary contributions	$4,000,000,000	$5,000,000,000
Passive income (investments, rents)	450,000,000	650,000,000
Active business income	400,000,000	1,200,000,000
Government funds (OEO, Hill-Burton Hospital funds, etc.)	2,565,000,000	4,435,000,000
Miscellaneous (wills, community funds, Bingo, raffles, etc.)	800,000,000	1,500,000,000
	$8,215,000,000	$12,785,000,000
ASSETS		
Stocks, bonds, investment real estate	$9,000,000,000	$13,000,000,000
Commercial business property	4,000,000,000	12,000,000,000
Personal property	500,000,000	900,000,000
Religiously used real estate	40,588,000,000	54,277,600,000
	$54,088,000,000	$80,177,600,000

Note: Reprinted by permission of the publisher from Martin A. Larson and C. Stanley Lowell, *The Churches: Their Riches, Revenues, and Immunities* (Washington, D.C. and New York: Robert B. Luce, 1969), p. 232.

The Roman Catholic Church

It may come as a shock to some Catholics to discover that their church is worth an estimated $80 billion and handles about $13 billion in cash every year. A further breakdown gives us some of the following facts: in 1970 the Catholic church spent $1 billion on new buildings.[12] Women's religious orders have an estimated wealth totaling $12.7 billion, and men's orders have $11.2 billion.[13] The Archdiocese of New York has a net worth of $643 million, of which $563 million is tied up in buildings and land.[14]

In general, as with Protestants, the bulk of Roman Catholic wealth is represented in property. For example, the church has 24,000 church buildings, 12,694 chapels, 788 general hospitals, 124 seminaries, and 13,000 elementary and secondary schools.[15] The bulk of the church's stocks and bonds seem to be held by the religious orders, who have established portfolios and hope to use the income for the care and support of aged members.

A look at the balance sheet for the New York Archdiocese may give us a better picture of how the Catholic church uses its wealth. According to its own financial report, the Archdiocese had a net income of $14.2 million in 1968. The money came from the following: Catholic Charities drives, $3.8 million; contributions, $3.0 million; tuitions, $4.4 million; investments, royalties, interest, $3.0 million. The largest item among its expenditures was for education ($11.6 million), with health and welfare services coming second. The Archdiocese ran in the red that year—$1.2 million, to be exact. In 1971 its deficit was $1.6 million.[16]

Not all dioceses give financial reports but from those which do it appears that the church is running in the red. Baltimore, for example, lost $1.5 million in 1969. La Crosse, Wisconsin, on the other hand, had a $2 million surplus.[17]

Nino Lo Bello, a journalist who crisscrossed the United States for months to get a true picture of Roman Catholic wealth, has this to say about his findings:

No matter where I travelled in America I found the same thing. The churches were hurting for money because their education programs had become too expensive. . . .

Before I set out to do the research on this book, I too had been awed by the "wealth" of the church. But I found that although the American Catholic Church does indeed possess substantial visible riches, it does not have cash. Essentially the church is land rich but money poor. . . . Moneywise, the American Catholic Church is in a bad fix. Many of the dioceses are on the brink of bankruptcy, and there is growing doubt whether the church can in the foreseeable future do anything to greatly improve its position.[18]

The Protestants

Statistics on the wealth of the major Protestant denominations are scattered and lack a common accounting procedure. Every year the National Council of Churches puts out a yearbook of church statistics, and recently it has asked for financial data. For the 1974 yearbook some thirty-nine denominations replied, reporting a total contributed income of $4.6 billion.[19]

In another survey conducted by the National Council of Churches, several denominations attempted to estimate their total worth. Many complained that this was difficult, since it meant compiling data from thousands of local affiliates. Again, the basis for data collection was not uniform, but some self-estimates of wealth were: Disciples of Christ, $652,061,674; Lutheran Church of America, $1,321,297,636; United Methodist Church, $4,846,378,956. (The Methodists also figured their total indebtedness: $571,462,030.)[20]

The National Council of Churches' yearbook notes that religion receives a major share of the charitable contributions collected in the United States: 43 percent of the total given in 1972, for example, or $9.75 billion. The next largest recipient is health services, with $3.68 billion in contributions.[21]

One final set of statistics from the yearbook that will prove of interest has to do with the annual expenditures for the construction of new religious buildings (table 8).

The figures show that new church construction reached a high in 1965 and has been declining ever since. If the recent figures are adjusted for inflation (using 1967 as the base),

Table 8
ANNUAL VALUE OF NEW CONSTRUCTION
OF RELIGIOUS BUILDINGS

Year	Value in Billions
1955	$ .736
1960	1.016
1965	1.207
1967	1.093
1968	1.079
1969	.988
1970	.931
1971	.813
1972	.844

Note: Reprinted by permission of the publisher from *Yearbook of the American Churches, 1974,* ed. Constant H. Jacquet, Jr. (Nashville and New York: Abingdon, 1974), p. 263

then 1971 commitments total only $.625 billion and 1972 expenditures total $.607 billion, or about half what was being spent in 1965. While this chart presents itself as carrying figures for "religious buildings," it seems unlikely that religiously sponsored schools or hospitals are included in the figures. Another source estimates that the Catholic church alone spent $1.45 billion on churches and other buildings in 1964, for example.[22]

Looking at some of these Protestant denominational studies, we might well wonder whether any of the financial data has been productive of consternation in the Protestant community. Has there been any outcry of alarm among sensitive observers? Not particularly. The socially concerned Protestant journal *The Christian Century,* looking at church assets in 1967, saw nothing objectionable in this financial picture. On the contrary, they were pleased that the churches had accumulated a few dollars and expressed the hope that the money would be used to influence companies' employment and racial policies through careful and moral investment. "In general we are confident that investigators will find practically no fat-catting [in the churches]. . . . For example, one major Protestant denomination recently had to turn away an able applicant for a minor editorship, for in order to match the applicant's 'secular' salary it would have had to pay him more money than the church's chief executive was getting."[23]

IN SEARCH OF HOLY POVERTY

Our review of church wealth in America has shown that, on paper at least, the church is a very rich institution. Most of its wealth, however, is tied up in land and buildings; and as church representatives are quick to point out, the value of these buildings is often reckoned in terms of what it would cost to erect a similar structure today, not what they may have cost in the first place.

We have seen that one observer, expecting to uncover vast amounts of church wealth, was surprised to find that the Roman Catholic sector is mired in the deficits arising from its school programs; and that a respected Protestant journal felt that there was scarcely any "fat-catting" in the church. But what is fat-catting? Certainly if we were to compare the operational standards of the American church with those of a business enterprise, we might find that the church was modest in comparison. Nevertheless it remains true that our standards for evaluating the church's wealth should be found, not in relation to the predominant style and expectations of our affluent culture, but in relation to Scripture and to the Christ we acknowledge as Lord.

I am aware that in my view of the church's present situation I am influenced by my own historical perspective. For it seems to me that when the early church began to amass wealth and to build costly places of worship, especially after it became, with the conversion of Constantine, the state religion, it was deflected from the course set for it by its Founder. In being a propertied institution, whether the established religion or not, it is inevitably exposed to the danger of becoming conformed to the world and allied to its centers of power. This seems to me to be, to some extent at least, the case today.

However, I recognize the validity of the arguments adduced by those who view the church as an institution with a social mission exercised through its wealth and property. To such a mission the development of schools, nursing homes, and hospitals might at times be perfectly justifiable. But the trouble is that institutions respond too slowly to change, and the pace of change in the last quarter-century is unparalleled in history. So the question is whether the needs the church is trying to serve with its immense "plant and equipment" are the urgent needs of today's society. It was not too long ago that much of the building connected with the church's social program seemed legitimate and even called for. That is not true today, and yet the building continues, in America and many other parts of the world. If nothing else is clear, it is evident that if Christ should return to earth today, he would find himself heir to an astounding amount of real estate.

In Pakistan a family of seven must feed themselves on one dollar a day; all around the world, millions are starving. And yet in this country and in the world at large, Christians systematically pump billions of dollars into property. What effect does this have on our ministry, our credibility, our ability to speak and act prophetically? What effect, indeed, does it have on the health of organized religion itself? Recent years have witnessed a falling-off in church attendance. As one commentator states the problem:

Surely it is one of the tragedies of our time that, as man's survival depends more and more on moral direction, the institution on which he has depended for that direction grows more impotent. . . . Segregated, insulated, narcissistic, rich, the average American denominational institution, like other vast institutions in society, has come to seem both impersonal and impervious to individual influence, breeding a feeling of anomie compounded of superficiality and frustration.[24]

The editors of *World Outlook,* a leading Methodist journal, agree: "It is the feeling that the church is a machine, not a community, and that the machine is running us, not we the machine."[25]

I remember a commentator saying that in Jesus' time the city of Jerusalem had several gates so narrow that they were called "Needle's eyes." When a loaded camel approached one of these gates, the load had to be removed before the camel could pass through. It doesn't seem impossible that Jesus was thinking of this when he said it would be easier for a camel to pass through the eye of a needle than for a rich man to enter heaven.

Imagine, then, our church trying to pass through the narrow gate leading into the City of Peace. Can we see it as a camel, loaded with treasure? More like a caravan stretching for miles and miles outside the gates, as far as the eye can see, laden with its burdens of riches. It does seem, doesn't it, that there might be a slight traffic tieup?

NOTES

1. Martin A. Larson and C. Stanley Lowell, *The Churches: Their Riches, Revenue and Immunities* (Washington, D.C. and New York: Robert B. Luce, 1969), p. 232.
2. Alfred Balk, *The Religion Business* (Richmond, Va.: John Knox Press, 1968), p. 44.
3. Ibid., p. 9.
4. *Christian Century,* June 3, 1967.
5. Balk, *The Religion Business,* p. 46.
6. Cited in Larson and Lowell, *The Churches,* p. 220.
7. Balk, *The Religion Business,* p. 9.
8. P. 185.
9. Nino Lo Bello, *Vatican, USA* (New York: Trident, 1972), p. 84.
10. Larson and Lowell, *The Churches,* p. 185.
11. Ibid., p. 201.
12. Lo Bello, *Vatican, USA,* p. 85.
13. Larson and Lowell, *The Churches,* pp. 222 and 224.
14. Lo Bello, *Vatican, USA,* p. 62.
15. Larson and Lowell, *The Churches,* p. 33.
16. Lo Bello, *Vatican, USA,* p. 62.
17. Ibid., pp. 54, 63.
18. Ibid., p. 211.
19. Constant H. Jacquet, Jr., ed. *Yearbook of the American Churches, 1974* (Nashville and New York: Abingdon, 1974).
20. D.B. Robertson, *Should Churches Be Taxed?* (Philadelphia: Westminster, 1968), pp. 163, 164.
21. Jacquet, *Yearbook,* p. 248.
22. Robertson, *Should Churches Be Taxed?,* p. 170.
23. October 4, 1967.
24. Balk, *The Religion Business,* p. 35.
25. Ibid.

9. The Church and Worldly Goods

In the preceding chapter we surveyed the situation of the Christian church in the U.S. today with respect to wealth. We shall now try to get a glimpse of the inner attitude of today's Christians toward worldly goods. David M. Knight, a Jesuit brother writing in the *New Catholic World,* tells a story that will begin our investigation in a humorous vein:

In that totally different world of twenty years ago, the children of poor black families surrounding our novitiate used to come to our kitchen for food. A brother would distribute the leftovers from the community meal. One day a child asked him:
 "Brother, how much they pay you here?"
 "Oh, they don't pay me anything. I have a vow of poverty."
 "What's that?"
 "Well, that means that anything I want, I go to the Father Superior and ask for it—food, clothes, money for a movie, and so forth—but I don't get paid."
 "You mean, anything you want, you just ask for it, and they gives it to you?"
 "Yes, that's it."
 "And what you call that?"
 "That's a vow of poverty."
 A long silence . . .
"Brother, where can I get me one of those 'poverties'?"[1]

Of course, this child might well be speaking for all the poor of the world. When we advance confidently on the project of simplifying our lives, we would do well to bear in mind that whatever we manage to achieve in that line is likely to have little connection, in this land of plenty, with the desperate daily struggle for survival experienced by the masses of dispossessed whose condition we examined in the earlier chapters of this book. Later on, we shall have more to say about poverty as a Christian practice; but first, a little more on the subject of what some have called the church's "edifice complex."

The typical American parish minister, reports Alfred Balk, a journalist who has interviewed many clergy, is under constant pressure from the church's congregation to do two things: increase the membership ("numbers signify success") and build or renovate ("building signifies progress").[2] American church congregations, Balk found, believe very strongly in a growth-oriented and success-oriented church:

Consequently, today whenever one moves from one community to another, he is apt to discover: (1) the church is in the midst of a major capital fund drive; (2) it has just completed one; or (3) it is about to embark on one. And this drive is likely to be for the purpose of (1) building an entirely "new, modern, and adequate church plant" at a recently acquired site; (2) extensively renovating the existing plant, including perhaps a new organ, central air conditioning, new youth rooms, a chapel, and sizeable off-street parking facilities; or (3) raising the money needed to complete such projects. . . . [3]

The relationship that can exist between the church and the rich and powerful, and its bearing on the construction of new buildings, is well illustrated by the case of Francis Cardinal Spellman, the former Archbishop of New York. When he first came into office in 1939, he made a point of getting to know every influential person in the business world of New York. "He made a practice of staging regular luncheons or dinners for bankers, financiers, real estate men, Wall Street brokers, business editors, corporation executives, labor leaders and other solid personalities in the world of business and commerce." These connections paid off. In time, he was able to cut the diocesan debt through the shrewd advice of his friends, and in 1945 he announced a building campaign which, by the end of his term of office (1967), amounted to over $400 million worth of construction.[4]

A funny story went into circulation which was printed in *Fortune* but is said to have had its origin in the Vatican itself. Cardinal Spellman, so it goes, dies and presents himself at the pearly gates, announcing himself as "a simple parish priest of nearly two million souls." Both he and St. Peter are surprised when his name is not to be found under that heading in the official files. So the Cardinal notes that he is the author of several articles and a book and suggests that perhaps he is listed under that category. But St. Peter still has no luck. Then, "reluctantly, the Cardinal pointed out that he had, among other things, built fifty churches and two hundred schools, as well as hospitals, homes for the aged and other charitable establishments too numerous to count. So for the third time Saint Peter went off, but this time he came back with a beaming smile. 'Come right in, Frank,' he said apologetically. 'We had you under Real Estate.'"[5]

HOW POOR IS HOLY POVERTY?

Do not store up for yourselves treasure on earth, where it grows rusty and moth-eaten, and thieves break in to steal it. Store up treasure in heaven. . . . Therefore I bid you put away anxious thoughts about food and drink to keep you alive, and clothes to cover the body. Surely life is more than food, the body more than clothes (Matt. 6:19–20, 25–26).

One of the greatest surprises I received as a national organizer for the Shakertown Pledge was the number of grateful and enthusiastic responses we got from Roman Catholic priests and nuns. Having been raised a Protestant, though baptized a Catholic, I knew very little about Catholic orders. My impression was that all priests and nuns took vows of poverty, chastity, and obedience; and I had assumed that the members of religious orders—those who are called the "religious"—practiced a rule calling for austere poverty. I was soon to learn otherwise.

I began to ask questions of every priest, brother, and sister I met, and what I learned was this: that secular priests are not expected to take a vow of poverty; and that among those who do—namely, the members of religious orders—a distinction is made with reference to whether their role in the church is "active" or "contemplative." In the case of the active communities, whose apostolate consists in, say, teaching, nursing, and the like, the vow of poverty is less literally interpreted than in the case of the contemplatives, whose apostolate is that of prayer and spiritual direction. Human nature being what it is, the rules can be rather liberally interpreted and, I understand, often are (especially among the men).

This is what is reflected in the anecdote with which our chapter opened. Brother David Knight's group, the Jesuits, is of course in the active category, and its lifestyle might well present a marked contrast to that of, say, the Carthusians or the Trappists. At the moment the Jesuits are in the midst of a debate about the true meaning of poverty. Some members of the order, he reports, are arguing that religious poverty is not to be interpreted as literal, material poverty but rather as "communal sharing and simplicity of life," or "availability" (the "poverty of time"). Of course, individuals vary widely in the extent of their material needs and their desire for material comforts, and for some the practice of "poverty of time," carried to the extent that one's time could never be considered to be one's own, would be vastly the more difficult. Nevertheless Brother Knight feels that these definitions are a "charade," an attempt to take the substance out of the vow. As an instance of this, he produces the example of the religious faculty of a Catholic university which "recently voted to put teeth into its vow of poverty by going on the budget plan":

Each member of the community would draw only a certain amount of money each month for personal expenses. Since board, lodging, medical insurance, prescription drugs and major medical expenses, annual vacation expenses (plus an annual visit home), one annual professional trip, and an annual retreat, laundry, dry cleaning, extraordinary travel expenses, and ordinary supplies (like toilet articles, stationery and stamps), use of the community's car, whiskey every evening and all the beer one could drink were not incuded in the budget, but were provided free by the community, the budget could afford to be modest. Seventy dollars a month was considered to be sufficient.[6]

Needless to say, Catholic religious differ on this point both as communities and as individuals. For example, Brother

Knight mentions a nun, living on the same campus, who sends all but $150 of her monthly salary to her motherhouse. Her rent comes to $90 a month, which leaves $60 for all other expenses, including food, toiletries, and travel.

Most Protestant ministers in America have not had to contend with the question of formal vows of poverty, yet clergy of all denominations have until very recently been expected to live in modest circumstances. Modest circumstances is, of course, a relative concept (like voluntary poverty), and while some clergy live fairly simply, others find that their rent-free parsonage, their tax breaks, their expense accounts, and their salary combine to permit them to live very comfortably.

I was recently part of a team that conducted a weekend retreat for fifteen Methodist seminarians and their wives. Many of them were already aware of the global situation and had begun thinking about their own lifestyles. As the workshop proceeded, a number expressed their uncomfortable feelings about the style of life they would enter upon after their graduation. Well-furnished parsonages and starting salaries of $10,000 were part of that style, as were expense accounts for entertaining members of the congregation and running a church plant of a large, expensive kind. They all wanted to think about moving into a simpler lifestyle, but as they considered the options (communal living, vegetarian eating, voluntary cuts in salary) they felt that the pressure of the congregation's expectation would prove too much for them. "What will I do when the bishop comes to dinner," one young wife blurted out, "serve him soyburgers?"

THE THEOLOGY OF SIMPLICITY

Early in the development of Christian teaching with regard to possessions, the distinction was made between those called to live according to the counsels of perfection—"Go, sell your possessions, and give to the poor . . . and come, follow me," as Jesus said to the rich young man—and those whose vocation was to remain the conscientious stewards of their wealth. Given that Jesus numbered among his following people like Joseph of Arimathea (a man of substance wealthy enough to

have a family tomb), there is scriptural support for this position. Its proponents argue that Jesus, seeing into the young
man's heart, was warning him of the danger of *attachment* to
his wealth as constituting a barrier between him and God, to
whom he wished to give himself completely.

But however legitimate the distinction between those to
whom Jesus' radical call was addressed and the lay populace at
large, surely the kind of double standard which has developed
was never intended. By this standard Christians are divided
into those who, in the matter of possessions, seek to be in the
world but not of it and those who see nothing unchristian in
the acquistion of immense wealth from whatever source, so
long as they remain "detached" from it.

It is this latter argument which—when they become concerned at the thought of their wealth at all—many very rich
Christians use to justify their holdings. "You see all this?" a
devout man who once employed me said, pointing to his
factory. "If the Lord asked me to give it up, I would do it
today." I had no doubt that he was completely sincere. I
couldn't help wondering, though, just what sort of message
would qualify as a call from Jesus. Would a television
documentary showing the starving faces of African children
be a clear enough call? Or a challenge by an environmental
group that his business—making ornamental stone frontings
for pharmacies, stores, and homes—was wasteful of natural
resources? Or would it have to be some kind of "road to
Damascus" experience?

It is so easy for us to deceive ourselves about our detach-
ment. True poverty, says Fr. Henri Nouwen, is determined by
a radical openness, an emptying of the self. "The self-emptied
man is revolutionary in the real sense because he claims
nothing—not even his life—as his possession, and therefore
he can take away the false basis of war and violence by refusing
every compromise with possessions."[7]

One text concerning which there seems to be no interpreta-
tive controversy is Jesus' judgment speech, wherein he says
that on the Last Day the Son of man will separate people into
two groups, putting the sheep on his right hand and the goats

on his left. Then he will say to those on his right hand: "You have my Father's blessing; come, enter and possess the kingdom that has been ready for you since the world was made. For when I was hungry, you gave me food; when thirsty, you gave me drink; when I was a stranger you took me into your home, when naked you clothed me. . . . " "Then the righteous will reply, 'Lord, when was it that we saw you hungry and fed you, or thirsty and gave you drink, a stranger and took you home, or naked and clothed you. . . . ?' " And he will reply: "I tell you this: anything you did for one of my brothers here, however humble, you did for me." The whole passage (Matt. 25:31–46) should be required spiritual reading for our time.

Considered in this light, the requirements of the Shakertown Pledge for simple religious lifestyle are a matter of ethical necessity. The debate about the spiritual dilemma of how much wealth is permitted to a Christian could go forever unresolved, but the urgent need of a life of sacrifice and sharing is becoming apparent to all. And in our new circumstances those dedicated religious people who have struggled with the difficulties of voluntary poverty for years can be seen, not as interesting Christian experimentalists, but as people who have been pioneering for us all.

We have been discussing, during these last two chapters, the situation of the church with respect to wealth, and in the chapter that follows we shall turn to the question of how the church may be brought closer to the ideal of Christian poverty. But it is most vital to keep in mind that the church is not some kind of abstraction we can better formulate: In a real sense we are the church. And so we must take to heart these words of Archbishop Helder Camara of Recife, Brazil:

Our responsibility as Christians makes us tremble. The northern hemisphere, the developed area of the world, the twenty percent who possess eighty percent of the world's resources, are of Christian origin. What impression can our African and Asian brethren and the masses of Latin America have of Christianity if the tree is to be judged by its fruits? For we Christians are largely responsible for the unjust world in which we live.[8]

NOTES

1. "Religious Poverty: After the Charade," February 1973.
2. Balk, *The Religion Business,* p. 25.
3. Ibid., p. 27.
4. Lo Bello, *Vatican, USA,* p. 142.
5. Ibid., p. 139.
6. "Religious Poverty," p. 19.
7. *Pray to Live* (Notre Dame, Ind.: Fides, 1972).
8. Quoted in James E. Will, "Understanding the Impact of World-Wide Inequities," *Christian Century,* May 7, 1965.

10.   Toward a Poor Church in America

"All whose faith had drawn them together held everything in common; they would sell their property and possessions and make a general distribution as the need of each required. With one mind they kept up their daily attendance at the temple, and, breaking bread in private houses, shared their meals with unaffected joy, as they praised God and enjoyed the favor of the whole people. And day by day the Lord added to their number those whom he was saving" (Acts 2:44–47).

The world into which Christianity came was, like ours, beginning to fall apart. Today historians are speaking of the end of the modern world; the glory that was Rome was coming to an end as the primitive church was beginning. Today, among the young people in our universities, there is an extraordinary interest in the esoteric and particularly in the mysticism of the East (surprising, in view of the materialism of modern civilization); and we find these intellectual trends paralleled in the ancient world. By its very style of living, the church came into the ancient world as a revolutionary body—simple, communal, filled with zeal and a radical openness; and, though persecuted, the early Christians, we are told in Acts, were "all held in high esteem" (4:34). In modern society, which is in many areas undergoing a phase of radical

163

experimentation, it is not surprising that the earliest age of the Christian church should be exerting a special attraction.

In their exhortations to Christians on the subject of wealth, the Fathers of the primitive church might well be speaking to Christians of our own time. Thus St. Ambrose:

Nature has poured forth all things for the common use of all men. And God has ordained that all things should be produced that there might be food in common for all. Nature created common rights, but usurpation has transformed them into private rights [*On the Duties of the Clergy*].

So also Pope St. Gregory the Great:

Those who neither crave what belongs to others, nor give away what they have, are to be admonished to consider seriously that the earth, out of which they were taken, is common to all men, and therefore, too, brings forth nourishment for all in common. In vain, therefore, do those think themselves guiltless, who arrogate to themselves alone the common gift of God. . . . For when we administer necessities to the needy, we give them what is their own, not what is ours; we pay a debt of justice, rather than do a work of mercy [*Pastoral Care*].

It is St. Gregory's teaching that under the old law a person was condemned for theft; under the new law a person is condemned for failing to give to others.

St. Basil makes the same point:

The bread that you store up belongs to the hungry; the cloak that lies in your chest belongs to the naked; and the gold that you have hidden in the ground belongs to the poor [*Homilies*].

Today the vast majority of the people who call themselves Christians in the United States are wealthy beyond the dreams of most of the world's people. Whether we like it or not, we are the rich of the world, and all that Scripture and Christian teaching has to say about the sins and the obligations of the rich is addressed to us. So, when we hoard our wealth, when we indulge in a luxurious lifestyle—when our closets, say, are crammed with clothes we never wear—we are guilty of a kind of theft. When we permit, and even encourage, our Christian fellowship to continue with its vast building projects in face of the world's hunger, we are failing in our Christian witness and giving scandal to the world at large.

When we allow our government to waste hundreds of billions of dollars on "defense," and our corporations to pillage lands and waters and dominate the economies of Third World countries, then by our very failure to take corrective action we are guilty of perpetuating an immoral and ungodly social system.

I say all this not because I think that the majority of Christians are willfully or even wittingly immoral—let alone the question of whether I am myself guiltless!—but because I think the time has clearly come for us Christians to wake up to the global danger posed by our own lifestyle and to allow ourselves to be profoundly changed by the demands of the gospel.

THE CHRISTIAN RESPONSE

What then can we ask of our church and of each other? How can Christians address the global crisis in word and action?

First, as individuals *we can adopt a simpler, more ecological lifestyle.* If thousands, and presently millions, of Christians should take the initiative of responding to the gospel call for simplicity of life and call upon fellow Christians to join them, this commitment would shine as a ray of hope for the building of a just global society.

Second, *we can call upon our church to assume the leadership in moving toward a new, simple, ecological style*—one which expresses a sense of stewardship with respect to all the fruits of the earth.

Third, in the affluent countries, *we as Christians and as churches must call our nation to account.* The rich nations and peoples of the world must be challenged to reorganize their overconsuming economies and commit themselves to a standard of living accessible to all the earth's people. In the poor lands (and of course in the rich lands too, where there are still areas of shocking poverty), Christians and their churches must identify with and support the cause of the poor and the oppressed. Church teachings, church influence, and church resources must be employed to their fullest capacity on behalf of those who are suffering from our present world system.

Fourth, and finally, *Christians everywhere must unite with other people of good will to form and sustain an international movement for global justice.* This movement must be grounded in a commitment to the betterment of all the world's people and a recognition that the resources of our planet belong to all people equally.

Imagine the impact of such a series of developments. If American Christians and—beyond that—if the worldwide community of Christians were to wake up to the desperate need around us, if we were willing to change our own lifestyles and reorient our church in such a way as to place our influence and even our lives on the line for a just global society—what might the consequences be in the social and economic order?

What would the consequences be of an all-out effort on the part of Christians to redesign our global economy? What if we were willing to do it as the people of a "poor" church—one rich in spirit but poor in material goods?

The answer would have to be that this agonized, desperate, discouraged world would receive a thrill of new hope —perhaps one strong enough to enable the world's people to pull together and forge a new global society in which starvation, premature death, and economic misery would be things of the past.

There are many who might argue that this is utopian, but the plain fact is that unless we are willing to be utopian, unless we are willing to dream of and work for a society very different from the one we have today, then we will condemn the majority of the world's people to lives of endless and deepening poverty, and we will find our own children growing up in a polluted, dangerous, morally abominable world.

If we are not able to forge a society that feeds the hungry and clothes the naked, it will not be because the resources aren't there. It will be because people were unwilling to let themselves hope and lacked the courage to take the risk. And therefore this call. A call for Christians to be people of courage. A call for Christians to be people of hope. A call for Christians to step boldly into the arena of political and economic strife and, where others have despaired, to bring healing and hope and love to a ravaged world.

In my conclusion (chapter 12) I will have more to say about Christian participation in an international movement for global justice. In the remainder of this chapter I would like to explore the idea of a "poor" or simplified church and share with the reader some of the signs of hope that are beginning to appear in the Christian community.

NEW VOICES FOR A NEW CHURCH

One of the most exciting developments on the religious scene today is that there are a great number of voices calling for a new Christian lifestyle. Many of these people have been willing to begin with their own lives in the process of their call for transformation.

"There cannot be justice for all as long as anyone consumes more than one needs," says Art Gish, a writer and a member of the Church of the Brethren. "Overconsumption is theft. We privileged people are the major source of the world's problems and they will not be solved before we give up our privileged position."

Cornell professor Richard Baer, Jr., environmentalist and New Testament theologian, says:

Should we in America refuse to alter our lifestyle, I believe we will experience increasing dehumanization—*of ourselves*—both individually and corporately. To begin to share on a broad scale, therefore, is not just a matter of obedience to God or of altruism but rather a necessary requirement for remaining human. We know what the gas chambers and crematoria did to the soul of the German people during the Hitler period. But we face a similar fate should we turn away from the agony and despair of our fellow human beings.[1]

And Jesuit priest William R. Callahan has urged the Catholic clergy to consider "more modest lifestyles, a movement toward simpler residences and recreation, more sharing with and availability to the people, speaking out as a voice for the poor and powerless. . . ."[2]

The beauty of these statements is that they are backed up by action. Art Gish, for example, lives in a simple community in the hills of Tennessee. Richard Baer was an originator of the Shakertown Pledge. William Callahan lives communally and works collectively with the Center of Concern in Washington, D.C.

As I have traveled around the country, talking and meeting with people about the Simple Living witness, I have discovered that Christians who are convinced of the importance of simplicity are also convinced that their church has got to change its affluent, unecological, and ostentatious style. In general, their views can be divided along two main lines of thought. The first would call for the *radical divestiture,* in fact the *deinstitutionalization* of the church, in accordance with the principle that the church should not own anything. The second would call upon the church to move toward a *radically new institutional style,* one simpler, more ecological, and more in general harmony with the world's needs. I shall try below to set out the major lines of argument for each position. Each, as will be seen, possesses real merit, and I suspect that as the movement toward simplicity develops, Christians will choose a course somewhere along the lines set out by these two positions.

Radical Divestiture

As we have said, the guiding principle in the divestiture movement is that the church should not own anything. Proponents of this position point out that the early church was content to have its meeting in the homes of Christian families; small "house churches" could again become the model for Christian worship. They believe that as the church divests itself of its wealth and secular power it will become open to a far greater power, that of the Holy Spirit operating in its members. The power of this renewed church would be in its *witness*, in its *example*, and in its *words*. "Holy poverty," said Cardinal Lercaro at the Second Vatican Council, "means that the church should follow Peter, who said: 'Gold and silver have I none, but what I have I give you.' " The advocates of a propertyless church hold that the church was never meant to have gold and silver and that what it has acquired it should promptly give away to a worthy cause.

Let's start with an inventory of the kinds of property the church now possesses and talk about how it might be given away.

Real estate. All houses, homes, apartments could be deeded over to their present residents or sold. All churches, schools, camps, shrines, and land could be given over to the people of the surrounding community for shared use, or given to the people who might be potential users of the property, or sold.

Stocks, bonds, businesses. All stocks, bonds, notes, etc., could be sold, or transferred directly to worthy causes. Businesses could be turned over to the complete control of their employees, or sold.

Pension funds could be turned over to the collective control of the people who have paid into the fund.

Schools and hospitals could be turned over to independent boards.

Art, sacred objects, murals, etc., could be entrusted to museums or special committees who would see to it that these treasures were preserved and put on display for all to see, or they could be sold.

All contracts to build, renovate, raze, could be cancelled, and any penalty fees paid.

Employees, pastors, and assistants could be kept on salary until the divestment process was complete. All would receive decent severance pay as programs were closed out. Beginning immediately, employees would be asked what their current needs are. From then on all payment should be according to need, and not based on seniority, grade, or department.

The money derived from such a divestiture would be given

to the poor and dispossessed, here and abroad, and to programs that operate in the political arena to change our international economic structure. Church programs regarded as of substantial benefit either to the community here or on an international scale could be independently chartered. This might have the salutary effect of combining the multiple interdenominational programs that now work in the same fields. Local communities of Christians might support out of their own pockets people whom they wanted to undertake special tasks in the sphere of social service or the ministry. (But watch out for this one, or soon there will be an institution all over again.)

Perhaps, the advocates of divestiture argue, such a revolutionary change would have the consequence that Christians could begin to look beyond their buildings and programs and to hear the real call of God in our time. Perhaps such a poor church could rediscover what William James, in his *Varieties of Religious Experience,* called the deeper significance of poverty, which consists in a liberation from material attachments, an "unbribed" soul, "the paying our way by what we are and do and not by what we have, . . . in short, fighting moral shape."

A Radically New Institutional Style

The second school of thought, also in favor of a poor church, would nevertheless oppose divestiture and deinstitutionalization out of a variety of considerations. First, they point out that an institution is the normal vehicle for the transmission of the cultural and religious values of civilization. This is not the first century, they say, and what is needed now is not a return to the primitive church. They advocate the development of a modern, focused, simplified church that could provide a model for institutions in the new society. They believe that we are in an age of large institutions wherein the church could play a significant role by organizing itself along lines of ecology, democracy, and global orientation.

While admitting that the Bible stresses the surrender of

possessions, this group points out that it stresses stewardship as well. Could not the church, then, lead the way in responsible stewardship? The advocates of this position consider themselves to be more pragmatic than those calling for divestiture, with particular reference to the following: A completely divested church would not be able to utilize the resources available to the organized church today; there is no guarantee that monies given away through divestiture will be put to better use than if they were retained by the church and simply diverted to programs more in line with society's present-day needs; as an organized force, churches are better equipped than other humanitarian groups to make themselves heard and felt with respect to moral issues in society.

Some of their concrete suggestions for church reform are these:

A moratorium on all new church building and, at the same time, the gradual release of underutilized church properties and the merger of existing church facilities.

A determined ecological focus in all church use of resources. This would mean drastic cutbacks in the use of paper, energy, office materials, space, slick publications; also a better use of existing church resources—opening church yards for the planting of gardens, for instance, and church buildings to fuller community use.

Subsistence salaries and simpler lifestyles for the clergy and for church employees. This would mean that those who elect to work for the church would accept the necessity of living according to a simplified lifestyle and would not expect to be keeping up with other "professionals" or with the church's middle-class congregants. It would also mean less jet travel, less money spent on conferences and gatherings in expensive hotels.

Increased emphasis on global justice and a simplified lifestyle as part of church programs. Such programs of instruction are of vital importance if the church is really going to change and to constitute a witness in the political sphere. Careful and sensitive work with congregational groups will be necessary if more than a small minority are to be persuaded to consider a real change in their lifestyle.

Other suggestions include moving out of elaborate national and regional headquarters, the selective sale of church properties, and the redirection of church pension funds and purchasing power to influence corporate policies in the areas of social justice, employment practices, and ecology.

There we have two arguments: one for radical divesiture and deinstitutionalization; the other for radical reorganization to produce a church capable of serving as a model for institutions in the new society. Both proposals have merit and can claim biblical sanction, and both are worthy of serious consideration and implementation. Either course, if pursued in earnest, would produce a church quite different from that of today, a church that could not be identified with the rich and powerful, either in style or in budgetary dependence, and might well be able to supply new leadership for a currently leaderless world.

SIGNS OF HOPE

From small prayer meetings to large interdenominational gatherings, from the mountains of Washington state to the plains of New Jersey, from Houston, Texas, to the Vatican in Rome—everywhere there are signs, to be observed in newspapers, magazines, and church bulletins, that Christians are waking up to the need for a simpler lifestyle and a church which speaks directly to the needs of the poor.

Here are some examples:

—In Chicago, when the archdiocese announced a ten-year, $250-million building program, an ad hoc group of local priests challenged the entire concept in a public letter, saying that the plan "placed too much emphasis on organizational structure and outdated forms of the church."[3]

—In New York City, the former Episcopal Bishop, Horace W.B. Donegan, announced that there would be no further work on the Cathedral of St. John the Divine "until there is greater evidence that the anguish and despair of our unadvantaged people has been relieved."[4]

—In the state of Washington, the pastor of a small-town Lutheran church called the headquarters of the Lutheran Relief Service in New York to say that his congregation would soon be sending them a check for $100,000. "We decided to borrow the money," he told the astonished chief administrator. "We figured that we'd be willing to do it for a church addition, so why not for the world's starving people?"

—In Spokane, Washington, Roman Catholic Bishop Bernard J. Topel has elected to live in a small one-bedroom house, where he does his own housekeeping and in the yard of which he grows much of his food. He keeps his needs simple and has been able to give most of his personal money away; and in addition, of course, he has saved the diocese money by his lessened maintenance requirements.

The list could go on. What this begins to illustrate is that what had seemed to be the established pattern of the American Christian church is being challenged at a number of points. Protests and actions are occurring with increasing frequency. The global resource crisis and the worldwide problems of poverty and hunger are compelling motives for a new movement toward Christian simplicity that is gaining power.

Increasingly, leadership is emerging from the official representatives of the established churches. When the American leaders of sixteen major Protestant denominations met in the winter of 1975 to discuss the world food crisis, they included in their final resolution a call to the church and to Christians generally to adopt lifestyles of "creative simplicity." In Canada, the National Conference of Catholic Bishops have urged their people to simplify their lifestyles, reduce their food consumption, and contribute more of their surplus to the world's poor. They also urged Canadians to exert pressure on their government to contribute to a world food bank, to pay just prices to Third World producers, and to assist low-income Canadians through a redistribution of income.[5]

Pope Paul VI, in a 1974 message to the United Nations, called upon the governments whose representatives were assembled to discuss world problems regarding development and the availability of raw materials to fashion "new, more just and hence more effective international structures in such spheres as economics, trade, industrial development, finance and the transfer of technology." He also appealed to the citizens of affluent countries to adopt "a new lifestyle that will exclude excessive consumption."[6]

Finally, the international religious gathering on global justice held in Aspen, Colorado, in June 1974 (which included in its attendance such figures as the former president of the World Council of Churches, Eugene Carson Blake, Rabbi Marc Tannenbaum, Fr. Theodore Hesburgh of Notre Dame, and the Most Reverend Marcos McGrath, Archbishop of Panama) concluded its deliberations by proclaiming "a commitment, not merely to bring immediate relief to the suffering, but also to work toward the creation of global structures which will ensure basic dignity and humane existence for all people."

The text went on to say:

The emergence of these global structures of unity, goodness and freedom to which God calls us is today impeded by evil entrenched in the structures of our common life: economic, political, and social. Our task as religious communities is to join hands with people everywhere, especially with the poor, the powerless and oppressed, in a common struggle for the liberation of all.

The cost must weigh most heavily on those most able to pay—the affluent among the nations, the rich among the people. What is required is nothing less than a fundamental change of national policies, institutional and professional behavior, and personal patterns of living.[7]

Apart from the signs we have been discussing there are three Christian movements, here and abroad, which seem to me to be special causes for hope. They are the Charismatic movement and the Evangelical Social Action movement in the United States and the international phenomenon of Taizé.

The Charismatic Movement

The growth and development of what has been termed the "Charismatic" or neo-Pentecostal movement in mainstream

Christianity seems to me to be full of promise for the renewal of Christian spirituality. Characterized by ecstatic utterance (speaking in "tongues") and belief in a special religious experience called the "baptism of the Spirit," it represents a return to Scripture and a strong emphasis on its teachings. It differs from the Pentecostal movement which began at the turn of the century in that it has not, for the most part, alienated its members from their denominations but has instead become a reform movement of growing strength and importance in a number of mainstream churches. Charismatics claim a membership of some 500,000 in the United States—mostly in the Catholic, Presbyterian, Episcopal, and Lutheran churches—and a large and growing international following.

As one who has visited and worshipped in a number of Charismatic gatherings around the country, I can attest to the vitality, the power, and the sheer excitement of this new outpouring of the Holy Spirit in our times. Many Charismatics have a wonderful sense of joy and peace and a radical trust in the power of the Holy Spirit to transform their lives and the lives of others. Of the Charismatics I have met, many are middle-class and Middle American in background, many are priests, nuns, ministers, academics—people, in other words, I would have expected to find adhering to more conventional forms of worship—but they participate fully in the excitement of this radical movement in which they are associated with so many others unlike themselves. This gives me hope that Christian worship will be able to break the bonds of culture and class, bringing a new unity among those dedicated to lives of service.

A particularly stunning example of what can happen is the Episcopal Church of the Redeemer in Houston, Texas. In 1965 this was a dying church in a dying neighborhood. Locked up tight six days a week, it managed to have only one service on Sunday, and the continuance of even that was in doubt. Then something rather remarkable happened. A new rector came and a small group of people committed themselves to the effort of renewing the church. And the Holy Spirit began to move in their midst with most powerful effect.

Now, ten years later, the church is totally and radically transformed. It is open seven days a week with youth groups, Bible classes, healing services. On Sunday its services are jammed. It has gone from having one full-time pastor to having a team, which in turn is backed up by an extensive and energetic lay ministry. Over four hundred of its members have made a total commitment to each other and to the ministry of the church, putting their worldly possessions into a common pot, living together in communal households, supporting each other in lives of service and healing. Because of this communal—and simple—lifestyle, some thirty people have been freed to work in the public school across the street (and they have transformed it from a racial hotbed into a model for the city); another thirty have gone to work in a nearby health clinic.

Wherever I travel in the United States I hear about the Church of the Redeemer. For the Charismatic movement it has become a kind of Mecca—a model, a home, a source of inspiration. The total dedication of its members, their willingness to surrender material goods and personal careers for a life of Christian service, has kindled a hope in the hearts of Charismatics and non-Charismatics alike that a powerful resurgence of the Spirit could occur in our country and in our church.

Many Charismatic communities have begun to follow the example of the Church of the Redeemer. In Ann Arbor, Michigan, the Catholic Word of God community has some six hundred members at last count, most of them living in "households." The majority of households do not engage in income sharing at present, but recently the household of each elder began to hold goods in common. Leaders expect this trend to carry into the whole community. Charismatic communities of size also exist in South Bend, Indiana, and in Cincinnati, Ohio. There one can find the same trend toward communal living, pooling of resources, and simplicity.

The guiding force behind this simplification of lifestyle and sharing of resources is not in the main a concern about the world's poor people. Rather, households have been deemed valuable because of the greater contact with other Christians and the greater chance for support and prayer. Pooling of resources has occurred so that more people and more time could be freed for the demands of Christian ministry.

One cannot help but wonder: What if, in addition to the very real spiritual benefits of simplicity and sharing, Charismatics came to believe that the conditions of our global society made an *ethical* demand for simplicity as well? What if simplicity, renunciation of material goods, and a commitment to Christian social action in the world arena became "fruits" of the Charismatic movement just as important as speaking in tongues, healing, and prophecy are today?

The Evangelical Social Action Movement

Recent stirrings within the "evangelical" wing of the American Protestant church also give rise to an expanded sense of hope for a relevant Christian witness in our time. "Evangelicals" are Christians who believe in the Lordship of Jesus Christ over all the affairs of their lives, who regard the Bible as the "authoritative" word of God, and who stress the experience of repentance and salvation in the life of a true Christian. They are, in other words, the theologically "conservative" branch of the Protestant church. They have also in recent times tended to be politically conservative as well. Some people have estimated that there are over forty million Evangelicals in the United States, which is not surprising since they include the Southern Baptists—the largest Protestant denomination in the country.

Many people are no doubt aware that the main force for social reform among Christians in the twentieth century has come from the liberal Protestant and Catholic denominations. For the most part, Evangelicals have been the backbone of social, economic, and political conservativism in this country. But it wasn't always that way. Professor Ron Sider, a dean at Messiah College and the founder of "Evangelicals for McGovern" in 1972, likes to point out that Evangelical Christians were in the forefront of the antislavery movement in America. Dr. Sider takes pains to make people aware that many prominent nineteenth-century evangelists—of whom Charles Granson Finney, the founder of Oberlin College, is a prime example—equated true salvation with the adoption of a proper Christian position on the slavery question (not that that was the sole requirement). Many of the significant reforms that occurred in prisons, aid to the poor, child labor laws, and education for women in the nineteenth century can be traced to the reform impulse that spread from the evangelistic crusades of that period.

Today there is a new movement among Evangelicals that is highly critical of Christian acquiescence in and conformity to the prevailing social standards with regard to affluence, racism, and war and is calling for a new biblical emphasis on social justice in this country and in the world. "Young Evangelicals" like Jim Wallis (editor of *The Sojourner*), Sharon Gallagher (Evangelical feminist and editor of *Right On*), and Richard Pierard (author and college professor) have been joined by more established Evangelicals like Carl Henry (founding editor of *Christianity Today*) and Dale Brown (former Moderator of the Church of the Brethren) in a new coalition to challenge Evangelical Christians to a commitment to social justice.

Calling themselves Evangelicals for Social Action, this group held its first workshop in Chicago in the fall of 1973. There a gathering of some one hundred members from around the country, including both blacks and whites, affirmed their commitment to Jesus as Lord and discussed what the consequences should be in their lives. "We cannot separate our lives in Christ from the situation in which God has placed us in the United States and in the world," they declared. The text of their resolution continues:

Although the Lord calls us to defend the social and economic rights of the poor, we have mostly remained silent. We must attack the materialism of our culture and the maldistribution of the nation's wealth and services. We recognize that as a nation we play a crucial role in the imbalance and injustice in international trade and development. Before God and a billion hungry neighbors, we must rethink our values regarding our present standard of living and promote more just acquisition and distribution of the world's resources.

The group also condemned racism and sexism and took a strong stand against the military bias of our government.

This statement of the Evangelicals quickly appeared in many of the leading Christian journals in the country, and many of the more theologically liberal Christians responded with surprise and delight. One group at the National Council of Churches drafted a response in which they admitted that while they themselves had been long on social action, they had been weak on personal commitment and prayer.

A year later the Evangelical group met again, this time to draft proposals for implementing their statement. Workshops and projects on the problems of hunger, peace, and social justice were planned or slated, and a strong and far-ranging Commitment of Economic Responsibility was adopted that speaks squarely to the question of Christian lifestyle.

Since many Christians have written to the national office of the Shakertown Pledge Group asking whether a specifically Christian version of the Pledge existed, I would like to reproduce the Evangelical Commitment in full.

A COMMITMENT OF ECONOMIC RESPONSIBILITY

I recognize that the earth is a gift of God, and that I am called to cherish, nurture, and provide loving stewardship of the earth's resources.

I affirm the Lordship of Christ over all of life, recognizing that he preached woe to the rich, asked that we lay not up for ourselves treasures on earth, and commanded that we pour ourselves out for the hungry, naked, sick, and imprisoned.

Through the power of the Spirit, and with the strength that comes from Christian community, I will seek to conform my economic life to the will of Christ.
Specifically:

1. I will seek to follow the example, teachings, and guidance of Jesus Christ in all my decisions about personal possessions and consumption.

2. I commit myself to live a life of creative and joyful simplicity and ecological responsibility, continually evaluating my standard of living in relation to my genuine needs and those of others.

3. I declare my solidarity with all people who are hungry, poor, and oppressed, and will share my personal resources with them.

4. I commit myself to work for the reform and renewal of the Christian church in the United States, one which is less enmeshed in its property and possessions, and whose abundance is available for the needs of the world's poor.

5. I commit myself to join others in bringing about a more just global society in which all people have full access to the needed resources for their physical, emotional, intellectual, and spiritual growth.

6. I commit myself to occupational accountability, evaluating the effects of my labor on human needs and well-being.

7. I commit myself to the creation of a radically new moral atmosphere, so that leadership in the church and the world may be able to make critical and costly decisions for human good.*

It is particularly interesting that there are increasing contacts between the Charismatic and Evangelical movements. Both groups stress the Lordship of Christ, both believe in total commitment and full discipleship, both find the Bible a central source of inspiration and teaching. If each group brought its full influence to bear on the other, one can't help wondering whether a new style of evangelism might result.

Imagine a new generation of evangelists, filled with the Spirit, manifesting gifts of healing, prophecy, and personal ministry and committed to simplicity of life and to global justice; a revitalized and socially dedicated Campus Crusade for Christ, or Inter-Varsity Christian Fellowship; a New Awakening in the church, sweeping not just this country but the Christian world and bringing with it a commitment to build a new society. At this stage it is hardly something to bet on, but it is certainly something to pray for.

Taizé

Lastly—and to me the most exciting of the events that inspire hope for the future—is a call for radical Christian simplicity issued in the fall of 1974 by a gathering of young

---

*For more information about the Commitment write to Steve Knapp, 1564 Edge Hill Road, Abington, PA 19001.

Christians, some forty thousand in number, at the ecumenical Protestant monastery in Taizé, France. The meeting which took place that September had been four years in preparation, a period during which there had been informal discussion, smaller conclaves, and the spreading of the invitation by word of mouth. The religious of Taizé were offered money by church bodies to assist them in extending hospitality to their "council of youth," but they chose instead to operate on a shoestring budget. In the end, their simple means and simple style were sufficient to gather dedicated Christians from around the world. Many of the young people (they ranged in age from eighteen to thirty, but there were also a good many older adults) came from Third World countries and were able to share with the assembly their first-hand experiences of repression, exploitation, and imperialism. But most members were from the affluent countries of North America and Europe. At the end of their three-day meeting, they issued a statement and a challenge that rings with truth. I would like to close this chapter with their call to Christian action:

We have been born into a world which for most people is not a place to live in. A large part of humankind is exploited by a minority enjoying intolerable privileges. Many police states exist to protect the powerful. Multinational companies impose their own laws. Profit and money rule. . . .

Numerous churches, in the southern hemisphere as in the northern, are spied on, interfered with, and even persecuted. Certain of them show that without any bonds with political powers, without means of power, without wealth, the church can experience a new birth, can become a force for liberation and radiate God.

Another part of the people of God compromises with inequality. Christians as individuals and many church institutions have capitalized their goods, accumulating vast wealth in money, land, buildings, investments. There are lands where the churches remain connected to the political or financial power structures. They draw on their superfluous wealth to give away large sums in development aid, but still make no changes in their own structures. Church institutions acquire highly efficient means of accomplishing their mission, of running their activities and bringing together their committees. But many discover that gradually life vanishes, leaving the institutions to turn over empty. The churches are more and more forsaken by people of our time. What they say is losing its credibility.

Whereas the Christians of the first period shared all they had. They gathered day by day to pray together. They lived in joy and simplicity. So they were recognized. . . .

Church, what do you say of your future?

Are you going to give up the means of power, the compromises with political and financial power?

Are you going to surrender your privileges, stop capitalizing? Are you at last going to become a "universal community of sharing," a community finally reconciled, a place of communion and friendship for the whole of humanity?

In each locality and over the world, are you in this way going to become the seeds of a society without class and where none have privileges, without domination of one person by another, of one people by another?

Are you going to become the "people of the beatitudes," having no security other than Christ, a people poor, contemplative, creating peace, bearing joy and a liberating festival for humankind, ready even to be persecuted for justice?

Church, what do you say of your future?

NOTES

1. "Poverty, Pollution, and the Power of the Gospel," *Stewardship*, vol. 26 (1974), p. 54 (a publication of the National Council of Churches).

2. "The Lifestyle of the American Catholic Church," *New Catholic World*, February 1973.

3. Balk, *The Religion Business*, p. 43.

4. Ibid., p. 46.

5. "Sharing Daily Bread," the Labour Day Message of the Canadian Catholic Conference, Ottawa, Canada.

6. Message to Dr. Kurt Waldheim, Secretary-General of the United Nations, April 4, 1974.

7. *Report from the Aspen Consultation on Global Justice, June 4-7* (Washington, D.C.: Overseas Development Council, 1974).

IV. SUMMING IT ALL UP

"I do not wish to seem overdramatic, but I can only conclude from the information that is available to me as Secretary-General, that the members of the United Nations have perhaps ten years left in which to subordinate their ancient quarrels and launch a global partnership to curb the arms race, to improve the human environment, to defuse the population explosion, and to supply the required momentum to development efforts. If such a global partnership is not forged within the next decade, then I very much fear that the problems I have mentioned will have reached such staggering proportions that they will be beyond our capacity to control."

—U THANT, UNITED NATIONS SECRETARY-GENERAL

11. Building a Movement for Global Justice

"My own picture of humanity today finds us just about to step out from amongst the pieces of our just one-second-ago broken eggshell. Our innocent, trial-and-error-sustaining nutriment is exhausted. We are faced with an entirely new relationship to the universe. We are going to have to spread our wings of intellect and fly or perish; that is, we must dare immediately to fly by the generalized principles governing the universe and not by the ground rule of yesterday's superstitious and erroneously conditioned reflexes."

—R. BUCKMINSTER FULLER,
OPERATING MANUAL FOR SPACESHIP EARTH.[1]

In my own grappling with the global situation I have tried to describe in this book, I have found that a good dose of R. Buckminster Fuller—with his optimism, his generous assessment of human capabilities, his delightful, innovative mind—is just the right antidote to the thick pall of gloom that seems spread by the writings of so many students of the present crisis. Therefore, as we begin this final section, the opening quotation seems particularly apposite. Buckminster Fuller has always felt that the greatest resource available to humankind has been our capacity for thinking things out, our amazing adaptability to new situations. While fully aware of the follies and failings of human history, he also believes that we are on the brink of great new possibilities in social and technological organization. That is optimism, yes; but I would like to point out that if the movement for global justice we are endeavoring to launch should succeed, the effect would be precisely that, for it would mean bringing humankind into right relation with our environment. With this in mind, I am going to start off by presenting a picture of global change, after which I shall suggest a few of the steps that might bring it about.

A PICTURE OF GLOBAL CHANGE

It is hardly necessary to point out that preoccupation with the inequities of our world economic system is not new in our generation; only the desperate urgency of our situation is new. When in 1948 Robert Hutchins, president of the University of Chicago, assembled a group of international experts to draft a model World Constitution, they recognized that global ownership of resources was an essential ingredient of any just world system. Thus they stipulated:

The four elements of life—earth, water, air, energy—are the common property of the human race. The management and use of such portions thereof as are vested in or assigned to particular ownership, private or corporate or national or regional, of definite or indefinite tenure, of individualist or collectivist economy, shall be subordinated in each and all cases to the interest of the common good.[2]

The principle of global ownership is obvious and of obvious value. Any intelligible plan for global justice will require the freedom to allocate resources on the basis of need. It simply can no longer be acceptable that private citizens, cooperatives and corporations, and nations should be allowed to assert complete authority over resources if these resources are needed by humankind.

But there is another requirement with respect to resources to which the draft World Constitution does not advert, namely, that the intellectual resources of humanity are also a common "wealth": Ideas should not be the property of corporations or nations but should be freely shared with all the world's people. In practice, this would mean the internationalization of all patents and the principle that ideas that are beneficial to humankind should be shared as rapidly and equitably as possible. Any corporation or nation which tried to assert ownership or absolute control over such knowledge would be acting unlawfully.

In principle the global ownership of resources—both natural and intellectual—would even now find considerable support among world thinkers and leaders. Putting it into practice, however, will be another matter. Global redesign will call for an international authority (or authorities) recognized and supported by the world's people which will have the power to direct the use of natural and intellectual resources for the benefit of all. Such an authority must be able to make long-range plans for the betterment of the world's people and the preservation of the world's environment. It must be able to spread the use of helpful technology and restrict the use of any that is harmful to the population or the environment. It must be able to plan for the exploitation of resources and develop mechanisms assuring a decent living standard for all.

To some people the power of such a world authority may seem staggering; and yet, is it all that much greater than the power at present exercised by the government of the United States and those of other nations over their territories and citizens? The important questions are how much power such a world government (or world institutions) will be given, how it will be constituted, and what safeguards will be provided for individual freedom. This is a discussion that any movement for global justice will have to enter upon in earnest. Both the dimensions and the details of the question are beyond the scope of this book; its solution will call for the knowledge and skills of the greatest of our international experts.*

---

*For an interesting discussion of an alternative to a strong centralized world government see George Lakey, *Strategy for a Living Revolution* (San Francisco: Freeman, 1973), chapters 7 and 8, especially pp. 186–196.

It is self-evident that the attainment on national and inter-national levels of a just global standard of living and of consumption—all the necessary changes in the global economy that we discussed in earlier chapters—will call for the placing of limits both upon nations and upon the popula-tions within their boundaries. How this might work out is best envisioned by a projection into the future. Imagine, then, this picture.

The year is 1986, and in this year the United States has been assigned a resource consumption quota that is two-thirds of what its consumption was in 1976. As part of a thirty-year plan of resource distribution and environmental harmonization, this quota will be gradually diminished until the United States is consuming approximately twenty-eight percent of what it consumed annually in the 1970s. Europe, Canada, the Soviet Union, Japan, Australia, and New Zealand have also been assigned progressively decreasing quotas. Certain scarce re-sources, such as petroleum and fertilizer, are being ap-portioned on a special basis, with preferential treatment being given to promoting agricultural development in the Third World. Meanwhile, all foreign holdings in developing coun-tries are being progressively nationalized or turned over to locally owned corporations. In some cases, compensation is paid to the expropriated owners by a special world fund; but in most cases payment is limited or even nonexistent, in accordance with rulings by international compensation courts based on evidence of a pattern of exploitation on the part of the companies involved.

In order to meet their quotas and provide equitably for the needs of their citizens, most developed countries have im-posed maximum personal consumption limits, or confiscatory taxation above a certain income level. Most capitalist nations among the developed countries have taken over public con-trol of their major corporations, in part because the corpora-tions have become bankrupt or in need of technological revi-sion, but mainly in order that limited resources can be utilized efficiently and without the added cost to society of profit-taking.

Most of the industrial countries have established guaranteed national incomes for their citizens. These, in combination with a new emphasis on the production of inexpensive and durable goods, have meant that a decent standard of living is available to all. Mass transit is rapidly replacing the automobile, and in many cases it is being provided free or at a subsidized rate. New industrial plants, with the latest anti-pollution technology, are being developed as part of a "green towns" program which is spreading middle-sized cities to previously underpopulated regions. Cooperative and family farms are being encouraged, since these are more susceptible of organic methods and utilize human (as opposed to mechanical) labor in greater proportion. Most countries have national and regional councils to encourage the arts, and the theater, music, dancing, and the plastic arts are flourishing. With the decline of the advertising industry, commercial television has changed drastically, and public and cultural programming is on the upswing.

Meanwhile millions of citizens in the developed countries are using their talents in new ways. Many, freed by the guaranteed national income, have volunteered for health, welfare, and other service jobs in their communities. Others are being trained for service abroad. Many educational institutions and systems are being developed or redesigned to provide training for social services, for the arts, and for the areas in which workers are needed throughout the world —engineers, medical technicians, agricultural advisors, and planners of all sorts. Many of the participants in these new training programs are middle-aged and older citizens who have returned for retraining in new fields.

On the international front, major disarmament pacts have been concluded, since most countries have realized that within the new world economy the cost of supporting the military is too great a burden. In most parts of the world, international tensions have decreased, and world travel and cultural exchanges are increasing. In the developing countries, major new projects in housing, industrial development, and agricultural production are underway. New international health programs are beginning to make real progress in the conquest of the major diseases, with medical care available to all the poor; and through the international food agency all but a small percentage of the world's people are receiving an adequate diet. An international literacy campaign has entered its second year, and the international community development corps has just announced that another one hundred million people will receive pure drinking water by the end of the year.

MOVING AHEAD

There are some who might feel that the above scenario is hopelessly utopian. My own feeling is that it is hopefully utopian. It is not presented as a blueprint for action so much as a vision to help shake loose our thinking.

One mental health expert has suggested that the impact of the present global situation on the human psyche "is like ten Industrial Revolutions and Protestant Reformations rolled into one and all taking place within a single generation."[3] He is pointing to the fact that the human species is poised at the edge of a monumental decision: whether we will seize control of our institutions and move with determination toward a just world society, or allow ourselves to drift into disaster.

The human predicament is such that effective action is going to have to be broad-gauged and radical—as radical as the scenario I suggest above, or more so. And yet such action is a possibility only if we are able to mobilize in the world a new movement, one inspired by the desire to save the earth for our own generation and the generations to come, whatever the risks in terms of sacrifice and temporary disorientation.

It is one thing to project a vision of global change. Launching a movement which might bring about global redesign is quite another matter. In my final chapter I shall try to suggest how such a movement might get off the ground.

NOTES

1. New York: Simon and Schuster, 1969, p. 59.

2. *A Constitution for the World* (Santa Barbara, Cal.: Center for the Study of Democratic Institutions, 1965), p. 28.

3. John Platt, "The Future of Social Crisis," in *The Next Twenty-Five Years, Crisis and Opportunity,* ed. Andrew A. Spekke (Washington, D.C.: World Future Society, 1975).

12. World Service

Let us imagine the formation of a new group on the stage of the world that might be called World Service. We can further suppose that this international organization has been put together by the joint effort of several major religious bodies, a few trade and professional unions, some regional and international service and advocacy organizations; and perhaps it even has the support of a few enlightened governments. It is founded on several basic assumptions: that the resources of the world belong to all the people of the earth, that all people have an equal right to realize their full potential, and that decisions about the allocation of global resources should be made by democratic bodies. Its program consists in launching and sustaining a global drive for redesign, and its initial efforts are directed at recruiting and supporting "world servers" from all parts of the world.

To this end it provides counseling and vocational advice for people who wish to develop their skills for world service. Its local offices stay in regular touch with such volunteers, and they are provided with on-the-job support, educational materials, field seminars, and opportunities for travel and work in foreign countries. But in particular they are assisted in orientating themselves with regard to the available opportunities for using their skills and knowledge in the worldwide project of building and sustaining a just global society. In other words, the role of our World Service group would be to locate, develop, and support a generation of people who have committed themselves to bringing about a new international order.

World Service doesn't have to be one big organization. It could easily be a common program undertaken by the many agencies and organizations now concerned with the world situation. The important thing is that a call should be sent out for people who are willing to put themselves on the line for a new world—and it will involve letting go of normal career expectations, living simply, seeing themselves as world citizens—and that when they have come forward they will get the support they need for their undertakings.

So far, so good. Now let us turn to the two main tasks that will face our international corps of world servers.

1. *Developing a coordinated plan for global redesign.* What is involved, of course, is a broad-ranging plan that has as its goal the provision of a decent way of life for all the world's people. The changed society I projected earlier will call for a multiplicity of undertakings to bring it into being. Ultimately it will require a thorough revision of the economies and institutional practices of the developed countries; a new international monetary system; a new trade system; national plans for re-shaping economies along equitable and resource-sparing lines; a clearly worked out and imaginative international program for the sharing of resources and the development of poorer regions; new technologies and new ideas about manufacturing or farming ecologically; new schemes for the production and distribution of food; new transportation systems. And as change progresses, the need will increase of revamping the educational and training systems and retraining and relocating workers whose jobs have been changed or eliminated. Plans must also be made for international technological sharing and nonviolent ways of resolving disputes.

What is needed at this stage, however, is not a detailed blueprint, but a plan which, though broad, is specific enough to inspire hope and new vision. Such a plan, with practicable ideas for every area of human activity, is an absolute necessity if global consensus for change is to be achieved. World Service could serve as the plan's coordinator, bringing together people who have developed expertise in particular areas and assisting them in developing new visions of their specialized fields in the context of a global plan for change. Many who are, for example, now trained in engineering, medicine, public communications, transportation, and manufacturing could be helped by World Service to use their knowledge and skills in the creative reorganization of the present structures in their area of competence, with a view to fitting these trades and professions into a larger scheme for global justice. Many who are about to choose a vocational area or are considering retraining for another job could be encouraged to develop global-planning skills in needed areas.

At this point the reader may well be inclined to say that surely in the United Nations we already have the organization equipped for the development of a global plan. That is true, of course, so far as facilities are concerned. But the problem is that at present the United Nations has neither the mandate nor the political freedom necessary for the undertaking of any program so inevitably controversial. It may be that in time the United Nations will be given the task of enlarging and clarifying such a plan, but it cannot be expected to initiate it. Furthermore, I will argue that the planning must be tied in with political action for global change, and it is unlikely that this would ever be regarded as within the United Nations' province. This leads us to the second task of our new group of world servers.

2. *Political action for global change.* Plans for global change are necessary and the process is exciting, but without determined political effort to bring about their adoption the undertaking will hardly be worthwhile. World servers, then, will have to see themselves as the catalysts and the organizers of a movement for global justice. This movement must be international in scope and membership, yet cognizant of local needs and problems. Its members must be willing to engage in lobbying, electoral campaign organizing, and prophetic and symbolic action; and it is not impossible that they will be called upon to engage in nonviolent campaigns of massive civil disobedience in the interests of global justice.

What we envision is something rather like the Civil Rights movement of the 1960s. Like that movement, the Global Justice movement will have to engage in all forms of political activity, adapting its strategies to the concrete situation; it will have to be constituted by dedicated people who are united in a common vision; it will have to be motivated by love of human-kind. But unlike the former movement, it will be played out on a global stage with global objectives, and it will challenge directly the power and prerogatives of not only private corporations but nations.

The work of this group can be carried on in various ways, depending on the political climate and the task that needs to be done: international petition and lobbying campaigns for the internationalization of resources, the running of candidates for national office who are global in perspective, perhaps, as Richard Falk has suggested, even the formation of a global political party that would run slates in national elections. Other types of activity are also possible: challenges to wasteful practices in the affluent countries, direct action campaigns (involving strikes, sit-ins, civil disobedience) to stop further military waste or halt support for repressive dictatorships, massive educational campaigns to change lifestyles, challenges to institutions like the church. All these and more could be components of a broad, courageous movement for global justice.

In contemplating such a group as World Service, we have been forced to be realistic about the obstacles it will meet and the sources from which resistance will come. Need we spell this out? Though our motive is love, it is not likely to be seen so by the multinational corporations, the leadership of nation-states or the military establishments within the various countries. It seems not at all improbable that all the resources for wielding power in the world which we described in the early chapters of this book might be brought to bear in opposition to such a movement.

The people of the developed countries, rich or poor, may be strongly opposed to any plan which limits national wealth and power—the rich particularly, who would face the reduction of their incomes and confiscatory taxes. The working classes—lower, middle, and upper-middle—may well feel threatened by proposals that might hinder their upward mobility or disrupt their jobs; the very poor may fear that a reduction of national production and consumption will mean that there will be even less to go around. And finally, many people will be opposed to the formation of an international authority or world government on patriotic, civil libertarian, or even religious grounds. In other words, the range of reactions may be formidable in the extreme: being denounced as traitors, communists, or agents of the devil is entirely within the realm of probability.

And yet, with regard to public opinion in the United States, the Harris Poll we cited earlier is of considerable interest. As reported in the *New York Post* of December 4, 1975, it indicates that around 77 percent of Americans are willing to simplify their lifestyle. And the questions, put to a cross section of the nation, including people at the executive level as well as white-collar personnel and skilled labor, have to do with concrete proposals like meatless days, wearing old clothes until they are worn out, cutting down on paper towels and plastic bags, driving cars a hundred thousand miles before junking them. It might be said, of course, that a poll reflects a mood of society that could change. But all the same it is noteworthy.

As I approach the last pages of this book, I am aware that it may be said that it is a book stronger on projections than on solutions. And that is true, of course. Given the magnitude of our global problems, it ought—within the inevitable limitations of its scope—to be true. But I hope that by writing it I shall have provoked thought and precipitated discussion. In an appendix I have provided lists of both books and periodicals which may be useful for further study leading to a broader and more expert understanding of our world situation than I have been able to convey.

For me the center of this book is the Shakertown Pledge, and that is further explained in the appendixes as well. I cannot but hope that my book will be heard as a call to action that will bring a multitude of new adherents to our movement for simple living and global commitment.

Lastly, as I said in my prefatory note, my inspiration for writing it—an inspiration of great urgency—came from a "time in the wilderness" in which I found my whole life clarified by the experience of Jesus. Today, it seems to me, the words Jesus addressed to the rich young man of the parable are addressed to all of us, whether we are Christians or not. For when he said we must love our neighbor, feed the hungry, and clothe the naked, he was not speaking to a handful of disciples in his own time nor even to the millions today who call themselves Christian: He was speaking to the whole world for all time. So, as Jesus was at the origin of this book, he should have the last word:

Jesus said to his disciples, "I tell you this: a rich man will find it hard to enter the kingdom of heaven. I repeat, it is easier for a camel to pass through the eye of a needle than for a rich man to enter the kingdom of God." The disciples were amazed to hear this. "Then who can be saved?" they asked. Jesus looked them in the face, and said, "For men, this is impossible but everything is possible for God" [Matt. 19:23–26].

APPENDIX A

WHAT IT WOULD MEAN
TO TAKE THE SHAKERTOWN PLEDGE

Many people are attracted to the sentiments expressed in the Shakertown Pledge but are not sure just what the Pledge might mean in their own lives. Here is a brief discussion of each item in the Pledge:

1. *I declare myself to be a world citizen.*

Recognizing that we are citizens of one world can have a profound impact on our daily lives. Those who make this declaration should begin to think of the needs of all the people of the earth and adjust their lifestyle, their social vision, and their political commitments accordingly. We must go beyond our familial, village, regional, and national loyalties and extend our caring to all humankind.

2. *I commit myself to lead an ecologically sound life.*

Through this we pledge that we will use the earth's natural resources sparingly and with gratitude. This includes the use of land, water, air, coal, timber, oil, minerals, and other important resources. We will try to keep our pollution of the environment to a minimum and will seek wherever possible to preserve the natural beauty of the earth.

Concretely, this should mean that we will participate in local recycling efforts. It means that we will try to conserve energy

199

and water in our own homes. It means that we will try to correct wasteful practices in our communities, schools, jobs, and in our nation.

3. *I commit myself to lead a life of creative simplicity and to share my personal wealth with the world's poor.*

This means that we intend to reduce the frills and luxuries in our present lifestyle but at the same time to emphasize the beauty and joy of living. We do this for three reasons: first, so that our own lives can be more simple and gracious, freed from excessive attachment to material goods; second, so that we are able to release more of our wealth to share with those who need the basic necessities of life; third, so that we can move toward a Just World Standard of Living in which each person shares equally in the earth's resources.

Concretely, those who take the Pledge should sit down with their families and review their present financial situation. Each item of expenditure should be looked at carefully, and unnecessary or luxury items should be reduced or eliminated. The surplus that is freed by this process should be given to some national or international group that is working for a better standard of living for the deprived. This surplus should be a regular budgeted item from then on, and each member of the household should endeavor to see how this surplus can be increased. In the future, families and individuals who have taken the Pledge might consider meeting together in "sharing groups" to discover new ways in which community and co-operation can free more resources for the poor.

4. *I commit myself to join with others in the reshaping of institutions in order to bring about a more just global society in which all people have full access to the needed resources for their physical, emotional, intellectual, and spiritual growth.*

This complements and enhances our commitment to share our personal wealth with those who need it. Wealthy nations such as the United States need to "de-develop" those parts of their economies that are wasteful and harmful in ecological and human terms. Wealthy nations must reduce their overconsumption of scarce resources while supporting the ecologically wise development of the poor nations to the point where the basic needs of all "spaceship earth" passengers are met equally.

We commit ourselves to use our political and institutional influence toward these goals. This means that we will support those candidates who will do the most for the poor both here and abroad. It may mean that we will engage in lobbying, peaceful demonstrations, or other forms of "direct action" in support of the transfer of more of our resources and skills to the developing lands. It means that we will oppose and attempt to change those aspects of our economic system which create an unjust distribution of wealth and power here and abroad. This also means that we will support efforts to bring religious, intellectual, and vocational freedom to peoples who are being denied basic human rights.

5. *I commit myself to occupational accountability, and in so doing I will seek to avoid the creation of products which cause harm to others.*

This most certainly means that we will not allow our labor to go into making products which kill others. It should also mean that we will take a close look at what we are producing to determine if it is safe and is ecologically sound. We should also consider our choice of a career, and whether it contributes concretely to a better world for all humankind. If our present occupation does not do so or is only marginally helpful to others, we may decide to change it, even if we earn less money as a result.

6. *I affirm the gift of my body and commit myself to its proper nourishment and physical well-being.*

Many of us in the developed (or "overdeveloped") countries desecrate the "temple" of our own bodies through overeating or through consuming physically harmful and nutritionally "empty" foods. Also, through our meat-centered diets we consume protein in its most wasteful form, depriving people in other lands of a desperately needed protein (see *Diet for a Small Planet,* by Frances Lappe, Ballantine Paperbacks).

Serious attention to this point would mean: (1) a commitment to maintain our weight at the normal health level; (2) a
reduction in the consumption of animal protein in our diets;
(3) regular attention to healthy physical excercise; (4) a reduction in consumption of empty calories, especially in "desserts,"
candy, pastries, alcohol, and other food products which contain great amounts of refined sugar.

7. *I commit myself to examine continually my relations with others,
and to attempt to relate honestly, morally, and lovingly to those around
me.*

We will seek to understand and improve our relationships
with others, and to treat each person as our neighbor. We will
try to affirm and nurture the gifts and talents of others. We
support the development of the small-group and face-to-face
community in religious life—since here many people are
learning new ways to communicate their love, their needs,
their hopes and dreams, and their anguish. Small groups and
communities have also been helpful in enabling people to see
more clearly how they affect others.

8. *I commit myself to personal renewal through prayer, meditation,
and study.*

For many people, "prayer" and "meditation" are alternate
terms for the same process of turning one's thoughts toward
God. We believe that deep and continuing personal renewal
can result from a discipline of prayer or meditation, and from
reading and reflection. We encourage all people to find their
own individual spiritual discipline and practice it regularly.
For a start, we would suggest setting aside time twice a day for
prayer or meditation.

9. *I commit myself to responsible participation in a community of
faith.*

We believe that God has a relationship not only with each of
us individually, but also with us collectively—as a people. One
of the obligations—and joys—of living our faith is that we are
called to worship together with others. We recognize that

common worship and the support of a community of common beliefs are essential to an active, creative, joyous life. Concretely, this means participation in a church or synagogue, or "house church" or other worship group.

Signing the Pledge

Taking the Pledge simply means that you agree with the substance of the nine points we have proposed and that you want to join us in a common community of support. The Shakertown Pledge Group is a loosely knit association of people who hold the principles of the Pledge in common and are attempting to redirect their lives toward creative simplicity and working for a more just global society.

The Shakertown Pledge was written to appeal to a broad audience composed of all people of faith. We encourage people from specific religious traditions to consider "writing your own pledge," in language that may be more uniquely suited to the language and practices of your community.

If you would like to join us in taking the Shakertown Pledge, please contact

National Office: The Shakertown Pledge Group
c/o Friends' Meeting
West 44th and York South
Minneapolis, MN 55410

If you would like to be on our mailing list, send us a check for $5 for one year. People on our mailing list receive *Creative Simplicity*, the monthly newsletter of the Simple Living movement.

APPENDIX B

QUESTIONS AND ANSWERS
ABOUT THE SHAKERTOWN PLEDGE

Here are answers to some of the most frequently asked questions about the Shakertown Pledge:

Does taking the Pledge mean that I have to give everything away and live in abject poverty?
No. Taking the Pledge means that you commit yourself to a process of simplifying your lifestyle. We expect Pledge signers over a period of time to move to a radically simplified lifestyle, but we recognize that people will have to proceed at their own pace. Pledge signers commit themselves to move toward a "just world standard of living" in which they are not consuming more than their fair share of the earth's resources.

Does taking the Pledge mean that I have to live a pinched, joyless life?
No. That's why we coined the phrase "creative simplicity." Pledge signers do not have to renounce the things that bring joy to life. They do not have to foreswear birthday celebrations, having guests for dinner, or occasionally going to the movies. Pledge signers should, however, search for alternate ways to celebrate and entertain themselves—ways that do not cost lots of money, or consume great amounts of fuel and energy. We particularly encourage people to find new joy in

community with others. Having friends over for a simple dinner and an evening of conversation and games is far less expensive than going out to dinner. Camping trips with family and friends are lots of fun, and cost much less than trips to Bermuda.

Do you feel that everyone should live communally?

Not necessarily. Many people who practice the simple lifestyle live in community, but that is not a requirement for a simple life. Some people who have signed the Pledge have been able to cut their expenditures by half while still living in a single-family dwelling, and we suspect that many others could do likewise. In the long run, however, community living is probably cheaper than living alone or in a nuclear family, and should be definitely considered as a possible lifestyle option.

Is it important actually to sign the Pledge?

Some people are philosophically or theologically opposed to signing pledges, yet feel that they want to "affirm" the lifestyle that is set out in the Pledge. Many others find that the actual act of signing the Pledge has real meaning for them. Either way, we in the national office would like to hear from you and know that you're "with us."

If everyone in the country adopted the Shakertown Pledge wouldn't that ruin our economy?

Our economy seems at present to be doing a very good job of ruining itself without any help from the Shakertown Pledge. We feel the Pledge represents ideas that should be the basis of a new, sounder economics: cooperation, ecological consciousness, concern for others, and simplicity.

Aren't you talking about revolutionary changes, then?

Yes, we are. A world economy based on sharing, and on meeting the needs of all the people would be a revolutionary development in human history.

Are you a political action group?

Not at present. We encourage people who have signed the

Pledge to get involved in ongoing political groups. There are already many groups that work for change on the local, national, and international level. Some of them are religiously based, some are secular; some work with legislatures, some with picketing and symbolic action, some with education and community-building. We do not try to prescribe our members' involvement and feel that people will get involved at the level that feels right for them.

We do, however, hold up a radical vision of what a new society could and should be. We will constantly prod our members to reflect on whether their current involvements will really help to bring about a new society.

Why do you mention God in the Pledge? Wouldn't it be better to have a humanitarian pledge that everyone could agree on?

The Shakertown Pledge is a call to the religious community to adopt a lifestyle that is in keeping with our Scriptures and our God. It was written by people who are seriously religious and felt called to challenge themselves and their affluent brothers and sisters. If a secular version of the Pledge is developed, we will welcome it.

Why don't you mention Jesus in the Pledge?

Because the Pledge is a call to all people of faith. If people feel the need, we see no reason why there shouldn't be a Christian Pledge, as well as a Jewish, Hindu, Moslem, or Buddhist Pledge.

I am interested in signing the Pledge, but I think my family isn't going to like the idea. What can I do?

Take the Pledge home and discuss it with them. Rather than laying out to them the reasons why *they* should take it, just share why it is important to you. If they are not willing to go along with it as a family unit, then try to figure out ways you can make changes in your own consumption and practices. In time they may join you. Trust the fact that this is an idea whose time has come, and that the Spirit works in many wondrous ways.

Parents tell us their children would never go along with the

Pledge, yet children are usually the most idealistic of all. Give your children a chance—don't lay the Pledge on them as a "law." Often children experience the simplicity idea as a restriction on their freedom; try to be aware of this dynamic.

What about the poor in our midst? Are you trying to get them to accept the status quo?

Absolutely not. People who take the Pledge are committed to working for a just global society "in which all people have full access to the needed resources for their physical, emotional, intellectual, and spiritual growth." We support the struggles of the oppressed to gain greater freedom, greater dignity, and assured access to the resources needed for a decent life.

If I take the Pledge, do I have to pay any dues? Is there anything I am committed to?

Taking the Pledge simply means that you agree with the substance of the nine points we have proposed and that you want to join with us in a common community of support. There are no dues. People who want to be on our mailing list and receive our newsletter, *Creative Simplicity*, are asked to contribute $5 per year if they can afford it. We hope to support our national organizing work from contributions by friends and signers of the Pledge, rather than by large institutional donations. Therefore contributions are welcome.

You talk about self-taxation and giving our surplus money to the poor. Do you have some ideas about where I should give my money?

We recommend *The Guide to Global Giving*, a pamphlet on stewardship and resource-sharing that does an excellent job of pointing toward truly effective giving ($1.50 plus postage from *Guide*, 4600 Springfield, Philadelphia, PA 19143).

Aren't you really organizing people by appealing to a sense of guilt?

We don't think so. It is true that affluent people often feel guilty when they face the gap between their lives and those of the poor. We doubt, though, that people will make a lifetime commitment like the Pledge on the basis of guilt. It is our experience that people take the Pledge because they feel it is the responsible thing to do and because they are already convinced that a simpler, more harmonious life is more rewarding.

Aren't the most important changes going to have to take place in the institutional arena? Isn't a lifestyle change really rather insignificant compared to a "structural" change?

Changing lifestyle by itself is not going to usher in the new society. But agitating for structural changes while still practicing an overconsuming lifestyle is simply hypocritical. Also, the level of consumption of food, energy, and raw materials by the affluent literally takes these goods from the use of poorer peoples. We feel that any significant movement for a new society must begin with people who are willing to live in consonance with their revolutionary values.

APPENDIX C

SELECTED BIBLIOGRAPHY, PERIODICALS, FILMS, AND AUDIO-VISUAL MATERIALS

The following reading list on simple living and global justice was prepared by Earl Pike of the Simple Living Collective in Minneapolis, Minnesota. I have added notes on some of the books used in the preparation of this manuscript.

Abbreviations:

CPC=Community Publications Cooperative,
 Box 426, Louisa, VA 23096.

III=International Independence Institute,
 West Road, Ashby, MA 01431.

BOOKS AND PAMPHLETS

I. THE GLOBAL SITUATION

The Limits to Growth. Donella H. Meadows et al. Signet. The highly influential report of the Club of Rome on world resources, pollution, population, and the prospects for a stable world order.

Man's Impact on the Global Environment. Report of the Study of Critical Environmental Problems. MIT Press. A study of resource consumption by a team of scientists based at the

Massachusetts Institute of Technology. Often referred to in the literature as "SCEP," this study provided the statistical basis for the *Limits to Growth* and other commentaries.

Resources in America's Future, H. Landsberg et al. Johns Hopkins. A Ford-financed study of America's consumption patterns, with projections for the year 2000. Completed in 1963. A good guide to our present and future consumption levels of energy, resources, etc.

The Environmental Side Effects of Rising Industrial Output. Alfred Van Tassel, ed. Heath. The report of a team that took the figures of *Resources in America's Future* and calculated the pollution and waste burden that they would impose on the environment. Published in 1970.

The Closing Circle. Barry Commoner. Bantam Books. Undoubtedly the best and most readable book on pollution in America. Biologist Barry Commoner takes a careful look at farming, lakes, and industrial production, assesses the problems, and discusses a national program for recovery.

An Inquiry into the Human Prospect. Robert Heilbroner. Norton. A world famous economist looks at the future and paints a gloomy picture of resource wars, pollution, and totalitarian governments—unless by some miracle we decide voluntarily to work together and make sacrifices.

The Hungry Planet. George Borgstrom. Collier. *Too Many.* Idem. Collier. *Focal Points.* Idem. Macmillan. Dr. Borgstrom is a nutritional expert at Michigan State University. His books provide an invaluable introduction to the complexities of the world food situation. If you could read only one book on food and food production, that book should be *Too Many.*

The Contrasumers: A Citizen's Guide to Resource Conservation. Albert Fritsch. Praeger. An excellent discussion of how Americans use resources, especially energy, and how we can conserve them. An appendix, "The Lifestyle Index, " gives ratings for the energy consumption involved in most of our daily activities and enables us to calculate just how much energy we are consuming.

The Trojan Horse. Steve Weissman and members of the Pacific Studies center and the North American Congress on Latin America. Ramparts Press. A superb and most enlightening collection of articles and essays on foreign aid and its misuse. Sections on the United States aid program, on the Food for Peace program, and military aid. Also sections on the World Bank and the International Monetary Fund.

II. Alternate Planning/Utopian Visions/Actions for Change

Mankind at the Turning Point: The Second Report to the Club of Rome. Mihajlo Mesarovic and Eduard Pestel. Dutton. A follow-up and elaboration of the *Limits to Growth* study. The authors argue for regional planning and a concept of "balanced development" in which the poor nations achieve greater growth while the rich nations cut back on wasteful consumption. Not nearly as much a blueprint of action as one might have hoped for.

The No-Growth Society. Mancur Olson and Hans H. Landsberg, eds. Norton. A good collection of essays for and against the concept of a "no-growth" or "steady-state" economy. A helpful introduction to what may be the most crucial debate of our time.

Design for the Real World. Victor Papanek. Bantam Books. A path-breaking discussion of technology and design in the twentieth century—how it is wasted and how it could be used to promote human welfare. Papanek gives enough new ideas and thoughts to make the reader realistically hopeful about the potential of human creativity in meeting world problems. This book deserves more acclaim and study than it has so far received.

The Pentagon of Power. Lewis Mumford. Harcourt. The concluding work in Mumford's survey of the development of Western civilization. In this volume he analyzes and traces the development of our attitude toward nature and the environment. He argues that unless we can regain touch with the human soul and with the rhythms of nature, we will be fated to perish in a neon desert.

The Chinese Road to Socialism. E.L. Wheelwright and Bruce McFarlane. Monthly Review Press. How the Chinese managed to feed their population and develop their country. A good analysis of regional and national planning mechanisms. A fine book to study for ideas about global planning and grass-roots development.

A Constitution for the World. Center for the Study of Democratic Institutions, Santa Barbara, Cal. A draft world constitution assembled by a group of experts at the University of Chicago. Provides a basic blueprint for world government.

The Environment Handbook. Garrett De Bell, ed. Ballantine. A special handbook prepared for the first environmental teach-ins in 1970. Good essays on the ecology problem on strategies and visions for change, and on tactics for political action.

Utopia or Oblivion. R. Buckminster Fuller. Bantam Books. *An Operating Manual for Spaceship Earth.* Idem. Simon and Schuster. Two excellent introductions to the works and thought of the world's foremost global planner.

Humanizing Our Future. The School of Living. Available from the School of Living, Rte. 1, Box 129, Freeland, MD 21053. $3.50. A transcript of talks by people in the forefront of social change and new visions. Includes talks by Paul Goodman, Helen and Scott Nearing, Mildred Loomis, Ralph Borsodi, Murray Bookchin, and others.

Bread for the World. Arthur Simon. Paulist Press. An introduction and action guide to the problem of world hunger. Its main thesis is that ordinary persons can help shape public policy. Simon is executive director of the organization "Bread for the World," an interdenominational citizens' movement on hunger and poverty.

Blockade! Guide to Nonviolent Intervention. Richard K. Taylor. Orbis Books. Dramatic case study of nonviolent action group's blockade of East Coast ports against West Pakistani ships. Includes a thorough, practical manual of nonviolent direct action.

The Community of the Future. Arthur Morgan. CPC (see abbreviations at the beginning of this bibliography). Morgan sees the small community as an essential component of human society and then proceeds to consider the conditions necessary for the development of communities.

Cooperative Communities: How to Start Them and Why. Swami Kriyananda. The author discusses the malaise of civilization and proposes cooperative communities as a solution, using his own community as an example of how to do it.

Strategy for a Living Revolution. George Lakey. Freeman. An excellent discussion of how a new society can be brought about through community experimentation, counterinstitutions, and nonviolent direct-action campaigns in the tradition of Gandhi.

Small Is Beautiful. E.F. Schumacher. Harper. A collection of essays from the man who coined the term "Intermediate Technology." A good guide to his thinking and to some of the values underlying his concept of economics.

Beyond the Rat Race. Arthur Gish. Herald Press. A fine argument for the adoption by Christians and others of simpler lifestyles. Includes questions and answers regarding lifestyle change with examples from the author's own life.

Begin at Start: Some Thoughts on Personal Liberation and World Change. Su Negrin. Times Change Press (order through Monthly Review Press). Negrin writes about her experience in various liberation movements (mysticism, free school, communal, new left, gay, feminist) and notes how they are all coming together.

III. LIVING MORE SIMPLY

A. Living in Community/Living on the Land

Living the Good Life. Helen and Scott Nearing. CPC. A fine narrative of how two people decided to live simply in the country and how it worked out.

Living Together in a World Falling Apart. Dave and Neta Jackson. Creation House. The Jacksons talk about what they learned from visiting Christian communities around the country. Child-rearing, money, decision-making, and so on, are discussed.

In Search of Utopia. Richard Fairfield. *Utopia, USA.* Idem. *Communes, Europe.* Idem. *Communes, Japan.* Idem. CPC. Overviews of the communal movement in many parts of the world. The people tell their own stories.

Gathered for Power. Graham Pulkingham. *They Left Their Nets.* Idem. Morehouse. Two books on the growth of the Church of the Redeemer community in Houston, Texas. This community has over 400 Christians living in cooperative households and giving an exciting ministry in the city.

Kibbutz: Venture in Utopia. Melford E. Spiro. Schocken. A historical analysis of a kibbutz first founded in 1920. Examines critically and sympathetically the issues of poverty, marriage, education, comfort, and communication as they have been dealt with over various periods in its life.

Clusters: Life Style Alternatives for Families and Single People. Paul Chapman. Available from Packard Manse, Stoughton, MA 02072, $1. A very helpful discussion of the isolated life in which many families and single people are caught and of how it can be changed through community. Written by someone who lives in a "cluster" himself.

The Joyful Community. Benjamin Zablocki. Penguin. A complete account of one of the most durable and successful experiments in community in this country. It details the life and times of the Bruderhof, a Christian society that began in Germany and now has three centers in the United States and one in England.

Journal of a Walden Two Commune. Twin Oaks community. CPC. The compiled newsletters of the Twin Oaks community tell the story of their experiment with a "behaviorist" community in rural Virginia.

Strange Cults and Utopias. John Humphrey Noyes. CPC. A history of all the known communal societies in nineteenth-century America. Noyes was the founder of the Oneida Community. A helpful book because it makes us aware that communal living is not new and also that it needs effort and vision.

B. Practical Tips

Household Ecology. Julia Percivall and Pixie Burger. Barnes and Noble. Positive, practical techniques and hints for the individual who wants to help save the environment. Includes topics like ecological shopping, detoxifying the medicine chest, recycling your discards, and teaching children a reverence for life.

The Natural Foods Cookbook. Beatrice Hunter. Pyramid Publications. A list of food sources, appliance suppliers for natural food preparation, and over 2,000 recipes.

Diet for a Small Planet. Frances Moore Lappe. Ballantine. Lappe gives an excellent introduction to the question of international food waste through meat-oriented diets and argues for an alternative grain-centered diet. Numerous recipes.

Recipes for a Small Planet. Ellen Buchman Ewald. Ballantine. A companion book for *Diet for a Small Planet,* giving a collection of tasty recipes.

Putting Food By. Ruth Hertsberg et al. The Stephen Greene Press. Readable instructions on drying, freezing, canning, smoking, and root cellars.

The Organic Directory. Jerome Goldstein and M.C. Goldman, eds. Rodale Press. A comprehensive list of organic food sources in forty-six states and Canada, complemented by essays on the state of natural foods today. Lists are included of the sources of natural fertilizers, of ecology and action groups, and of organic gardening groups.

How to Make It on the Land: A Complete Guide to Survival in the Country. Ray Cohan. Waldenbooks. A farming book for the city dweller.

The Home Health Handbook. Stu Copans and David Osgood. CPC. A resource book for home treatment of small illnesses and problems.

How to Build Your Own Furniture. R.J. Cristoforo. Harper. A wealth of information on techniques for quality furniture crafting.

The Illustrated Hassle-Free Make Your Own Clothes Book. Sharon Rosenberg and Joan Weiner. Bantam Books. A resource book for being comfortable, feeling good, and looking however you want to. This book gives you all the basic information plus patterns and ideas.

Source Catalogue #2: Communities. The Source Collective. CPC. This is a survival catalogue for living in urban communities.

Living Poor with Style. Ernest Callenbach. Bantam. *How to Live on Nothing.* Joan Ransom Shortney. Simon and Schuster. *The Penny Pincher's Guide.* Ellen Usher Durkin. Bantam. Three books on how to cut back, substitute, bargain, and in general live on less.

Directory of Free Schools. Directory for Personal Growth. Directory of Social Change. Available from Alternatives, 1526 Gravenstein Highway, Sebastopol, CA 97452. $1.00 each. Guides to groups and programs in three areas of self-help and new vision.

The Guide to Global Giving. Phyllis Taylor et al. Available from *Guide,* 4600 Springfield Ave., Philadelphia, PA 19143 ($1.50 plus postage). An evaluation and guide to the major international charitable organizations based in the United States. When you have saved a lot of money by living simply, this book will help you give it away to a good cause.

The Alternative Christmas Catalogue. Available from Alternatives, 701 North Eugene St., Greensboro, NC 27401. A resource book for life-affirming ways to celebrate Christmas, other holidays, birthdays, weddings, etc. Lists cooperative and self-help programs which produce goods for gifts, plus other ways to spend your money—or not spend it at all.

Working Loose: A Book About Finding Work You Want to Do. Available from American Friends Service Committee, 160 N. 15th St., Philadelphia, PA 19102. A fine book on alternative jobs and on creating your own job.

Design with Nature. Ian McHarg. CPC. If you are planning a community or a homestead, this book tells you step by step how to make the best use of your land both esthetically and ecologically.

The Community Land Trust: Guide to a New Model for Land Tenure in the United States. Available from III (see abbreviations at the beginning of this bibliography). This is the book that sets out the main arguments for a new and revolutionary form of landholding in the country.

Rural New Towns: Toward a National Policy. Simon Gottschalk. III. Proposal to establish rural new towns as alternatives to metropolitan regional migration for rural poor families.

This vision can be extended to planning for people who want to move from the city.

Planning A Rural New Town in Southwest Georgia. Simon Gottschalk and Robert Swann. III. Theory and practice behind New Communities, Inc., a 5,700 acre land trust in Georgia.

Community Development Corporations: An Annotated Bibliography. Florence Contant. Available from Center for Community Economic development, 1878 Massachusetts Ave. Cambridge, MA 02140. 50 cents. A guide to resources, books, and articles on forming and using a community development corporation.

PERIODICALS

Manas. A curious, serious, and sometimes insightful mixture of anarchist, theosophist, and modern psychiatric thought brought to bear on problems ranging from the education of children to the ending of war. P.O. Box 32113, El Sereno Station, Los Angeles, CA 90032.

Creative Simplicity. The newsletter of the Simple Living Movement. Tips, personal accounts, resources. $5.00 per year from Simple Living Collective, c/o Friends, Inc. West 44th and York South, Minneapolis, MN 55410.

The Green Revolution. Grandparent of counter-culture newspapers and magazines, publishing since the 1930s. Issues have dealt with pig slaughtering, rescuing trees, planting trees, defoliation, dandelions, and water wheels. $4.00 per year (monthly). Rt. 1, Box 129, Freeland, MD 21053.

The Mother Earth News The self-sufficiency magazine, a guide for the road to independence. $5.00 per year (6 issues). P.O. Box 38, Madison, OH 44057.

Country Women. A collective of women, many living communally, writing about aspects of living in rural environments and the problems and joys of women in that context. $7.00 per year (monthly). Box 51, Albion CA 95410.

The Leaves of Twin Oaks. Magazine of the Walden Two community in Virginia. $3.00 per year (bi-monthly). Louisa, VA 23093.

Natural Life Styles. A magazine covering the whole scope of natural living, with a special emphasis on food. $3.00 per year (quarterly). 53 Main St., New Paltz, NY 12561.

Wood Heat Quarterly. Vermont living, simple living, spiritual living. Practical, plain, and poetic all at once. Articles on fuel supply, mules, soil care, herbal medicines, water witching; mixed in with the philosophy of Kirpal Singh, Wei Po-Yang, and the Essene Gospel. $3.00 per year (quarterly). R. D. 1, Wolcott, VT 05680.

Work-Force. An excellent magazine put out by people who are living alternative lifestyles. Many, many listings in each issue about vocations for social change. $5.00 per year (bi-monthly). Vocations for Social Change, Canyon, CA 94516.

Consumer Reports. Articles on every imaginable product, plus lively pieces on various cases of marketing misbehavior. $8.00 per year (monthly). Mount Vernon, NY 10550.

Alternate Society. Source of news from communes. Political in nature, it relies heavily on reprints. $5.00 year (monthly). 47 Riverside Drive, Welland, Ontario, Canada.

Modern Utopian. Somewhat theoretical, occasional source of news from particular communities. $10.00 per year (quarterly). Alternatives, P. O. Drawer A, Diamond Heights Station, San Francisco, CA 94131.

Communes. One of the hardest-working, most effective of commune publications. $4.50 per year. Commune Movement, Dit, 141 Westbourne Park Road, London, W. 11, England.

Foxfire. A beautiful periodical on Appalachian lifestyle and craft. $6.00 per year (quarterly). Rabum Gap, GA 30568.

Anarchy. A left-anarchist publication. 29 Grosvenor Road, London, N. 9, England.

Liberation. A mixture of anarchism, socialism, and pacifism. Highly recommended. $7.00 per year (monthly). 339 Lafayette St., New York, NY 10012.

Catholic Worker. Nonviolent Christian anarchist newspaper. 25 cents per year (bi-weekly). 36 East First St., New York, NY 10003.

Roots: The Anarchist Ecology Magazine. A good perspective on problems of environment and development. $3.00 per year. P. O. Box 344, Cooper Station, New York, NY 10003.

Peacemaker. Pacifist-anarchist paper emphasizing personal actions, simple living, and draft/tax resistance. $3.00 per year (tri-weekly). 10208 Sylvan Avenue, Cincinnati, OH 45241.

Win. One of the best magazines on the left, *Win* stresses revolutionary nonviolence and the affirmation of joy. It is put out from a communal farm in upstate New York. $7.00 per year (weekly). Box 547, Rifton, NY 12471.

Resurgence. Published by a group of which E.F. Schumacher *(Small Is Beautiful)* is a member. Pursues the course of social change through nonviolent action and alternative lifestyles. $6.00 per year. 275 Kings Road, Kinston, Surrey, England.

Simple Living. An irregularly published paper containing articles and news items from the simple living movement. Subscription price: an occasional donation. Simple Living Program, American Friends Service Committee, 2160 Lake St., San Francisco, CA 94121.

FILMS/AUDIO-VISUALS

New York Newsreel. Radical, political, participatory, documentary and fiction, plus films from Cuba, Vietnam, Europe, and Japan. Write for their catalogue. 322 Seventh Avenue, New York, NY 10001.

Diet for a Small Planet. 28 min. color. $30.00. Good for people who want to know how to prepare meatless meals. Bullfrog Films, Box 114, Milford Square, PA 18935.

Looking for Organic America. $45.00. The first in-depth study of organic farming in the United States. At a time when farmers are being driven from the land each year by the high-priced machinery and toxic chemicals of agribusiness, organic farmers are demonstrating that ecological principles can be incorporated into profitable family farming. Bullfrog Films, Box 114, Milford Square, PA 18935.

Man and His Resources. 1960. 29 min. B&W. $14.00. Shows that a minority of the world's population uses most of its natural resources. Explores the responsibility of the haves toward the have-nots. Contemporary Films, McGraw-Hill, 828 Custer Ave., Evanston IL 60202.

For further information on the movement for voluntary simplicity readers are invited to write to:

Alternatives Resources Center
P.O. Box 1707
Forest Park, GA 30050
Phone (404) 361-5823